Before Victoria

BEFORE VICTORIA

Muriel Jaeger

1956

CHATTO & WINDUS

LONDON

PUBLISHED BY
CHATTO AND WINDUS LTD
42 WILLIAM IV STREET
LONDON WC2

★

CLARKE, IRWIN AND CO LTD
TORONTO

To
MARGARET A. PYKE
first reader and friendly critic

CONTENTS

INTRODUCTION

CIVILISATION is the great preoccupation of our time owing to the general fear that our own civilisation may be in its decadence. Crusted old humanists believe that the eighteenth century was the high point of this civilisation of ours and that it has been on the down-grade ever since. They hold that the decline began when the sweetness and light of the Age of Reason passed into the sombre earnestness of the Victorian Age. That some such change occurred is generally agreed; but what was the nature of the process? What happened in the lives and minds of the individuals of that time to make them turn away from the groves of enlightenment and gracious living to the prison of narrow conventionality and repression? At what stage in that strange transition did the younger generation begin to reproach its elders with frivolity, thus reversing the usual routine of the generations?

Having become interested in this problem, I began to investigate in a desultory manner, as time and opportunity allowed, and my search was presently stimulated by the discovery that precisely that phenomenon had occurred—the young reproaching their elders for frivolity—in the lives of several of those of whom we have records, and at about the same time. Encouraged, I went further and this book is an account of what I found.

The great events and movements that accompanied the change in morals, manners and tastes which took place in this country in the fifty years between 1787 and 1837 have been amply studied by many able writers. There were the French Revolution and the

Industrial Revolution. There were religious revivals, literary movements, scientific inventions, new philosophical and economic theories. But my curiosity was rather to know how the changes in thought and behaviour actually came about in the day-to-day lives of human beings.

How came it that Hannah More, who wrote successful plays in her youth and saw David Garrick act twenty-seven times in his last season, never entered a theatre in later life and wrote vehemently against its evil influence? Why had Miss Fielding's book for children to be re-edited in 1820 with the fairy-tales left out? What had happened to Voltaire's England, where there could be no Tartuffes, since 'for there to be religious hypocrites, there must be true devotees', when Dickens produced Stiggins and Pecksniff? What had become of the gentleman who advertised in 1792 for 'a curacy in a good sporting country where the duty is light and the neighbourhood convivial' when Wilberforce wrote in 1813 that 'the race of buck parsons is nearly extinct'? And under what stresses did Harriet Cavendish, daughter of the famous and notorious Duchess of Devonshire, write the pathetic little appeal to her brother, 'Pray, dearest Hartington, marry someone whom you will like to stay with'?

The people of the late eighteenth and early nineteenth centuries were highly vocal and greatly interested in themselves; they had the letter-writing habit perhaps more strongly than any other generation; many of them kept diaries; so that there is no shortage of material for such a study as I wished to make. On the contrary, to cover the whole ground would be more than a lifetime's work, and I have had to choose my lines of inquiry, not at random, but at some risk of overlooking evidence that might be important for my purpose. It has seemed more fruitful to concen-

trate, on the whole, on individual life-stories, sometimes of those who led in the new fashions; sometimes
of those who were caught up by them; of others who
might almost be called victims to them, and of a few
who resisted with varying degrees of success. Not many
of these have escaped the biographers; some appear
incidentally in the letters and biographies of others.
But a new understanding, I think, emerges from the
placing of them side by side.

Was this pervasive change, after all, a rise or a fall
in civilisation? The older humanists' view of the eighteenth century as the peak of European Society's
achievement is not universally accepted. And their
depreciation of the Victorian Age has become less
convincing to a generation sighing for safety and
homeliness. On the other hand, some philosophic historians of a wider scope believe that our decadence
began much earlier. Arnold Toynbee, though careful
to suggest that the situation may not even yet be
beyond remedy, thinks the trouble began centuries
before with the failure of the mediæval popes to fulfil
their high destiny. By his criterion, the widespread
return to strict Christianity during the period 1787–
1837 would no doubt represent a rally. Certainly the
loss in open-mindedness was compensated by a gain
in driving-force. But of these two qualities, the first is
the more civilised in all the usual meanings of the
term. I have, to the best of my capacity, left judgments
of value to the reader and confined myself to the study
of such evidence as I have found.

PIONEERS IN CONVERSION

*There are no Tartuffes in England. For there
to be religious hypocrites there must be true
devotees.*
                                    VOLTAIRE

WHEN a town is attacked by an invading
army, the people flock into the churches; and
one may surmise that they include many
who are not regular churchgoers. The *Annual Register*
of 1798 describes a similar phenomenon when 'the
irreligious and profligate doctrines by which the
French democracy sought to shelter the profligacy of
its conduct' caused a similar alarm in the 'upper ranks
of society' in England.

The churches were well attended [it says], and
sometimes even crowded. It was a wonder to the
lower orders throughout all parts of England to see
the avenues to the churches filled with carriages.
This novel appearance prompted the simple country
people to inquire 'what was the matter?'

But this article in the *Annual Register*, though written
within a few years of the event, was inaccurate when
it proceeded to attribute Royal Proclamations 'for
paying a decent and due regard to Sundays' to the
effect of the French Revolution. At least one such proclamation was issued in 1787, two years before the
French Revolution began and before any but a few
thinkers had foreseen any such devastating upheaval.
The agent behind this proclamation was William
Wilberforce, whose renown as the man who achieved
the abolition of the Slave Trade has obscured to some

extent his equally important rôle in the change in morals and manners which is the subject of this book.

At the time of the Proclamation, Wilberforce was twenty-eight. His conversion to what he considered to be genuine Christianity had occurred about two years before and had been a definite psychological crisis with the usual features of depressions, agonisings, solitary spiritual wrestlings and illuminations.

This particular conversion brought some consternation to a fairly wide circle, since, though middle-class by birth, Wilberforce had been adopted into London society owing to wealth, talent and a close friendship with William Pitt, the Prime Minister. He was one of the spirited young politicians who had swept into Parliament in that triumph of youth, the electoral victory of Pitt in 1784; and, as he had won by sheer eloquence the important county seat of Yorkshire against powerful vested interests, he was already a person of some consequence. Boswell had fortunately been present at the crucial meeting in York, and reported, 'I saw what seemed a shrimp mount upon the table, but, as I listened, he grew and grew until the shrimp became a whale.'

Like Bunyan and other religious enthusiasts, Wilberforce after his conversion adopted a somewhat exaggerated view of the sinfulness of his earlier life. He seems, on other people's evidence, to have been very moderate in his dissipations. No doubt, as he says, he wasted a good deal of time at Cambridge; young gentlemen almost invariably did in those times and, indeed, in most times. But he never drank heavily, and he gave up gambling early. However, as this sacrifice was not from motives of piety, but merely kindliness, because he could not bear to see other people lose more than they could afford, it probably appeared to his later self to have no merit at all. He certainly used strong language occasionally—a fact which caused some embarrassment to his differently reared sons when they came to write his biography in 1834. Writing from France in 1784, he exclaims, 'At last they are gone and the devil go with them!' The biographers' footnote comments on this passage, 'The propriety of inserting this letter unaltered will be manifest from the sequel'. The sequel was the conversion.

No allusion to any sexual licence in these early years is to be found in Wilberforce's own record, nor in any of his contemporaries; and no opportunity for scandal would have been missed by his bitter opponents in the Slave Trade campaign, if any had existed. In short, the unconverted Wilberforce must have been not merely a good enough sort of young man by the standards of the time, but better than most. He was most industrious, at least after the Cambridge days; he was in earnest in his political convictions, which, like Pitt's, were then of a liberal and progressive type; he retired frequently to his country villa at Wimbledon for quiet reflection. He had also social graces. He was far from handsome, or even robust, but he was a witty conversationalist; the Prince of Wales would go anywhere to hear him sing, and he was a clever mimic, though this indulgence he also gave up on the criticism of his elderly friend, Lord Camden, who thought it vulgar.

Few people, it seems, can have had less occasion to undergo a moral crisis and it is hardly surprising that the conversion came as a shock to his family and friends. It was not that conversions were rare in eighteenth-century England. About forty-five years before Wilberforce passed through his crucial experience, Wesley had set out on his first preaching journey through the country and, since then, conversion had become a very common occurrence among the English 'lower orders'. But, among their betters, it was not respectable; least of all, in the aristocratic society to which Wilberforce belonged and which set the tone for the country. Even before this time, the word 'enthusiasm' had become a term of opprobrium, having been specialised to describe this type of religious eruption, and the nineteenth century was well begun before it began to regain a sympathetic sense. One whole aspect of the subject of this book could be illustrated by the gradual change in the status of this word.

In spite of Voltaire, religious zeal had in fact never disappeared in England since the time of Cromwell's Saints.* It had become discredited at the Restoration, only to emerge again in force at the call of Wesley and Whitefield. But it could not have been more out of fashion; the upper classes knew better; they belonged to the Age of Enlightenment; and the rising and ambitious among the middle classes followed their lead. Most people practised a quiet conformity to the National Church—what Wilberforce later called disgustedly 'rational religion'. It was based, he said, on the idea that man is naturally good, though liable to error and weakness, while the devil was 'regarded as an evanescent prejudice which it would now be to the discredit of any man of understanding to believe'.

Thus, except for a few open agnostics among those in a position to flout convention, people in Society remained vulnerable. If anyone came to them with a Bible and a prayer-book and said, 'Do you really believe these things? If so, why don't you act upon

* Evidently Voltaire, though in some sense a revolutionary, cannot have mixed much with the 'lower orders' during his years in England.

them?', they had no answer ready. And if the question continued to be pressed loudly and persistently, they would presently have to decide whether they really were Christians or not.

But at the time of Wilberforce's conversion there existed no group large and strong enough to pose these questions loudly and persistently to the society in which he lived. There were, indeed, a few eccentric aristocrats, like the famous Countess of Huntingdon, who had taken up Methodism, just as others developed weird scientific theories like Lord Monboddo's belief that men were descended from apes, or engaged in absurd experiments like Lord Stanhope's attempt to drive ships by steam. But even the Blue-Stocking ladies, friends of Dr. Johnson, and themselves touched by the serious-mindedness which began to cloud over the latter end of the Age of Enlightenment, disapproved of Lady Huntingdon. Mrs. Montagu wrote of her in 1756: 'I believe and hope she means well, but she makes herself ridiculous to the profane and dangerous to the good.' There was also the Duke of Grafton, great-grandson of Charles II, who became the target of Junius through the extreme openness of his illicit love-affair while Prime Minister and his habit of cutting cabinet meetings to go to the races. In later life, he turned to theological inquiry and became a militant Unitarian, though, according to Arthur Young, his agricultural expert and a disciple of Wilberforce, he never attained a sufficient sense of sin.

These were the whims of ageing aristocrats who could afford to indulge them; Wilberforce in his twenties, confidant of the Prime Minister, with the world at his feet, was a very different matter.

However, in the upbringing of this influential young man, regarded as a member of the eighteenth-century upper classes, there had been a fatal flaw. His family, a rich commercial one in Hull, had held the usual easy, tolerant Christianity of the established Church. Counting his blessings in later life, Wilberforce listed 'to have been born an Englishman in the eighteenth century of decently religious parents with a fortune, talents, etc.'. But other allusions in his diary and letters are less indulgent. 'At least as much pains had been taken by my nearest relations and guardians, to make me dissipated and vain,' he wrote in 1822, 'and, though they did not mean it, vicious also, as are commonly used to counteract these dispositions.'

But Wilberforce's father died in his childhood and his guardianship was transferred to an uncle who lived in London. Between the ages of ten and twelve he went to school there, spending the holidays in his uncle's house, and it happened that his aunt was a great admirer of Whitefield and had Methodistical leanings. Since the Methodists had not at that time formally seceded from the Church of England, this was then possible, though hardly desirable, in a household of standing. Under this influence, the boy developed 'a rare and pleasing character of piety' and, as his biographers remark, no doubt acquired the 'habits of devotion which fostered that baptismal seed which though long dormant was destined to produce at last a golden harvest'.

To his mother, however, the effects appeared anything but promising; she descended upon the Wimbledon home and carried her son away in a whirl of indignation. 'You should not fear,' she told the protesting aunt, grieved at the loss of her proselyte. 'If it be a work of grace, you know it cannot fail.' Ultimately, it did not. Meanwhile, 'If Billy turns Methodist,' said his grandfather, 'he shall not have sixpence of mine.'

For the boy himself, it was a distressing wrench, but he was quite frank in his later account of the back-sliding that followed. Hull, he says, was then as gay a place as could be found out of London. He did not long resist the efforts of his family and friends to charm away his seriousness. They surrounded him with frivolous companions, they flattered and coaxed him, they took him to parties and they almost used force to get him to the playhouse. But they succeeded; and it was many years before the latent bitterness which always follows successful pressure on a young mind came again to the surface.

Later, Wilberforce saw the hand of Providence even in this lapse, since he might not otherwise have entered political life and been of service there, but would probably have become 'a bigoted, despised Methodist'. Certainly, the interlude between the lapse and the reconversion was valuable for his future career. He saw the Hand of God once again in the fact that he had not become a conscientious Christian at the time he won his Yorkshire seat, since, if he had, he could never have taken the necessary steps to win it.* Generally, the fourteen years of worldliness gave him an enormous advantage with the society in which he was to be a missionary. He learnt its manners, its ways, its mode of talk; he knew how and where to attack it.

Yet, with all allowance for this childhood influence, Wilberforce's conversion remains something of a mystery. So far as can be seen—and his own account is quite unguardedly open—there had been no disaster,

* These steps at the time involved large expenditure in various forms of bribery. At Hull, where Wilberforce had held the seat before that of Yorkshire the election cost him £8,000. A single vote cost two guineas—to be paid after the last day on which a petition could be presented. At York, his speeches turned the scale, but he would have had no chance without the usual forms of canvassing as well.

no misfortune, public or private, no emotional crisis of any kind. In the season of 1784, after Parliament was prorogued, he had appeared at York as the 'joy' of the races. Whatever that may mean, it does not suggest religious preoccupations. And he 'spent his twenty-fifth birthday at the top wave and highest flow of those frivolous amusements which had swallowed up so large a portion of his youth'. So write his solemn sons in 1834, adding immediately, 'Yet at this very time the providence of God was guiding him into the path which issued in his altered character.'

Such crisis as there was appears to have been a moral one. Wilberforce was brought up against the dilemma which he afterwards presented to so many others—the inconsistency between what he professed to believe as a Christian and the life he led. The agent in his case was Isaac Milner, a Yorkshire clergyman, whom, as a second choice, he invited to go abroad with him in 1784. Milner did not behave like one under the influence of Methodist views. He 'appeared in all respects like an ordinary man of the world, mixing like myself in all companies and joining as readily as others in the prevalent Sunday parties. . . . Had I known at first what his opinions were, it would have decided me against making the offer.'

Milner's own views seem at that time to have been purely theoretical and they came out gradually in the course of discussion. He appears, in fact, largely to have converted himself in the process of converting Wilberforce—which may well be the most efficacious mode of conversion. They travelled together again the next year, when they studied theological writings and then turned to the Greek testament itself.

Apparently, the results of this study came as something of a shock, to Wilberforce, at least. It seems clear that many otherwise educated people of the time really

did not know their Bibles * or what they were supposed to believe. Sir Joshua Reynolds had complained
not long before that viewers of his 'Infant Samuel' kept
asking him who Samuel was. Wilberforce, no doubt,
would have learnt that much in childhood from his
aunt and her friends, but it is unlikely that he knew
much of the doctrines of the Church. On the other
hand, no educated man, however much time he had
wasted at the University, could then have been ignorant of Hume and Voltaire; and no educated man
could have been unaccustomed to discuss all subjects
with freedom and detached curiosity.

One would expect that to such a man the suggestion
that he should believe in original sin, the devil, Hell,
Heaven, the rigid observance of Sunday as an absolute
obligation, and a man's disposition on his deathbed
as decisive for a blissful or an agonising eternity, would
seem the limit of absurdity. If a decision must be made,
it would seem that it must be that he could not be a
Christian. The reverse occurred. By the time they
reached Spa on the second journey, though Wilberforce says that they joined in the pleasures of the
English society there as usual, he adds, 'Mrs. Crewe
cannot believe that I can think it wrong to go to the
play—surprised at hearing that halting on Sunday
was my wish and not my mother's.' This recurrence
of the playhouse—nowhere forbidden in Scripture—
seems significant, especially as he was now with his
mother. At this time, he says,

> often in full enjoyment my conscience told me that
> in the true sense of the word I was not a Christian.
> I laughed, I sang, I was apparently happy and gay,
> but the thought would steal across me, 'What mad-
> ness is all this; to continue easy in a state in which a

* The author is well aware that this would apply also to
many otherwise educated persons of the present day.

9

sudden call out of the world would consign me to everlasting misery, and that when eternal happiness is within my grasp.'

In the late autumn of 1785, alone at Wimbledon, Wilberforce passed through the final turmoil of conversion. In those easy-going days, Parliament did not meet again until February and his time was his own. He spent it in study, prayer and attendance at religious services, avoiding social gatherings as much as possible. He had no intellectual doubts; he was convicted of sin, he felt the 'deep guilt and black ingratitude' of his wasted life and opportunities, and yet the notion that his feelings might change again constantly tempted him to avoid committing himself. He saw his alternative dangers—that he might draw back for fear of the scoffing audience he would have to face, or that, if he persevered, he might take a sinful pride in his resolution. He was constantly taking his spiritual temperature—a habit which became life-long—'read the Bible, too ramblingly, for an hour . . . very insensible and cold in the evening service—some very strong feelings when I went to bed . . . very fervent in prayer this morning', 'All religious thoughts go off in London', 'St. Anthony's—Mr. Forster's—felt much devotion and wondered at a man who fell asleep in the Psalms, during the sermon I fell asleep myself'. There is nothing to show whether the diarist saw any humour in this last entry.

The crux of the struggle came to be the question of open acknowledgment. In early December, he paid a secret visit to Newton, an unorthodoxly fervent clergyman who had once been a slave-trader. The secrecy was by his own careful arrangement—he pointed out that the faces of M.P.s were pretty well known. And yet, at the same time, he had decided on the method of direct dramatic announcement to his friends, and the letters were actually written before he saw Newton.

Their reaction was all that he had expected. Naturally they did not recognise the opening gun of the assault that was to destroy their pleasant, tolerant, open-minded society; yet such an aberration in such a person was an unpleasant shock. His mother was greatly distressed. Some of his friends comforted themselves that it could be only a temporary depression; one of them threw the letter on the fire. Others supposed that, as he seemed to them quite good enough already, he could only mean to retire from the world, as an ascetic.

Pitt took the matter seriously. It was indeed of some importance to him, absorbed as he was in political plans, for Wilberforce had included a warning that he might not in future be able to be as much of a party man as in the past. It must have been disconcerting to a Prime Minister to receive such an announcement from the member for Yorkshire and one of the best speakers in the House—one to whom he had once offered to postpone the opening of Parliament for a week or ten days, if it was important to him to stay in Italy a little longer.

In fact, the moment gave occasion for the young Prime Minister to display eighteenth-century open-mindedness at its best, and at its most vulnerable. Nothing of this kind, he wrote, could make any difference to their friendship. He knows Wilberforce's motives must be serious, but fears he may be deluding himself with principles which will defeat their own objects and render his virtues and talents useless to him and to mankind. He is relieved that Wilberforce denies that his religion is gloomy or that of an enthusiast. But why then this preparation in solitude?

He pleads for complete openness to one who 'does not know how to separate your happiness from his own'. If his friend will give him a chance to talk to him, he will not importune him.

Wilberforce's sons do not quote this letter in their biography; but they report the conversation that followed. Wilberforce agreed that he ought to conform to the world so far as 'a perfect duty to God, myself and my fellow-creatures' allowed. Pitt tried, he said, to reason him out of his determination, but soon found himself unable to find logical objections to it, if Christianity were true. This, of course, was the real crux, and Pitt was brought to admit that Bishop Butler's *Analogy* (in defence of Christian doctrine) had raised more doubts in his mind than it had answered. It seems that *his* answer to the question Wilberforce posed to himself and then to others must have been that he was not a Christian and could not be.

The children of the Age of Enlightenment were at a disadvantage when the converts attacked them, as the man who can see many sides of a question is always at a disadvantage with the opponent who can see only one. Pitt's conduct to Wilberforce was perfect and remained so throughout his life, often under extraordinary provocation. He never reproached him when the spirit moved him to upset vital political plans; he backed him about the Slave Trade in and out of season; he listened patiently, if without yielding, while he argued against the training of the militia on Sundays when Napoleon was encamped at Boulogne; he even maintained his friendship when Wilberforce's conscience most inopportunely came down against Lord Melville and eliminated the least dispensable member of his cabinet at the most critical moment of the war. He might almost be said to have forgiven his own martyrdom, since the loss of Melville threw such a weight of work and responsibility upon him that it certainly hastened his death. To Wilberforce, however, the tragedy of Pitt's death was that his friend had not been told of his danger in time for a thorough-going repentance. He said he would never forgive the Bishop of Lincoln, who was in attendance, for it.

The convert was no less fortunate with his constituents. They had been proud of their interesting and eloquent young member and of their own independence in electing him in the teeth of the great magnates of the county. But as the news of his conversion spread about, they began to have misgivings. His own protestations as well as a general rally among his local friends were required to reassure them that he had not become too eccentric to defend their interests. He was even forgiven for refusing the stewardship of the York races in 1790 and transferring his subscription to the County Hospital. In the long run, his conversion probably helped him to hold the seat until he retired of his own accord twenty-six years later; for, if his private life became duller, his public one did not. A religious zealot was then a rebel, and, if he was also an independent M.P., there could be no lack of picturesque and dramatic situations in his career; and Yorkshire has always cherished its original personalities.

Once the plunge was taken, Wilberforce lost no time, though it was twenty years before his conscience proved to have become so formidable that it could turn the scale in the ruin of a powerful cabinet minister. He was still a member of the established Church and remained so. Indeed, the fact that he stayed in it and did not join the Methodist secession may well have decided that the Church of England should survive. For, like the Catholic Church after the Reformation, the English Church was able to make head against the

disrupters only by developing an evangelistic movement in itself; and the first step was the Royal Proclamation of 1787 against Vice and Immorality. That
this step preceded the French Revolution by two years
clears eighteenth-century society of the charge that it
began its reformation only under the pressure of fear.

The Proclamation seems to have been almost the
single-handed work of Wilberforce; at least, this is the
impression conveyed by his sons. 'God', says his
Journal with magnificent audacity, 'has set before me
as my object the reformation of (my country's) manners.' This self-dedication seems to have preceded
slightly that to the Abolition of the Slave Trade and
thereafter the two objects were linked together as
Wilberforce's main purposes in life. Either alone seems
a sufficiently bold undertaking for one man, whatever
his advantages. Later, he regarded the French Revolution and the consequent wars as having retarded
Britain's moral progress. At this distance of time, it
seems doubtful whether his object would have been
attained at all without them. Undoubtedly, eighteenth-
century society would have put up more of a fight
against the new Puritanism. But at the time, Horace
Walpole remarked that the Proclamation was 'no
more minded in Town than St. Swithin's day'.

Horace Walpole, however, was always prone to
cynicism. More conclusive seems to be the general lack
of comment. Very little contemporary allusion to the
Proclamation is to be found. But it is natural that
Wilberforce's filial biographers should have made it
appear a far more effective step than other evidence
would lead one to suppose.

Possibly the Proclamation was regarded at the time
as no more than a conventional gesture of the Church.
From his advantageous political position, Wilberforce
had approached the Archbishop of Canterbury and,

through him, the King, himself a worthy grandfather
of Queen Victoria.* The Proclamation enjoined the
enforcement of laws already in existence against Sabbath-breaking, swearing, drunkenness, licentious publications, unlicensed places of public amusement
and the misuse of licensed places. The *Morning
Chronicle* of July 25th announced that the bishops had
gone into their dioceses, on a message from the King,
to give instructions to their clergy to co-operate with
the civil powers in enforcing these orders.

Again, there is no evidence that this move effected
very much; in fact, there is negative evidence that it
did not, in the long-drawn-out struggle that followed.
But, to Wilberforce, the real value of the Proclamation
was that it gave him a plausible pretext to form a
Society for the reformation of manners, which was at
first called 'The Proclamation Society'. This deft alibi
shows the value of a political training to a religious
reformer. He was quite frank about it to his friends.
He asks Lord Muncaster to keep his name out of it as
far as possible, lest the cause suffer through resentment
at his officiousness. But he followed up the bishops,
visiting six of them personally in the summer of 1787,
and enlisting many as founder members of his Society.

Such a Society was strangely out of keeping with
the spirit of the age which was just approaching its
end, though no one then knew it. The eighteenth
century was, above all, tolerant. As in our own times,
the laws against Sabbath-breaking and other pleasant

* Students of Victoriana may be interested in the style of
this despatch from George III to Addington, a Prime Minister
after the King's own heart—'His Majesty has received the box
containing the new appointment of Paymaster, as also that of
joint paymaster. The King cannot find words sufficiently expressive of His Majesty's cordial approbation of the whole
arrangement which *his own Chancellor of the Exchequer* has wisely,
and His Majesty chooses to add, most correctly recommended.'

peccadilloes were largely in abeyance; no one thought of enforcing them, apart from a few fanatics. An organisation which would encourage spying and laying information about breaches of them might have been expected to raise an outcry. Yet there seems to have been as little reaction as to the Proclamation itself; that came thirty-six years later, when the Society against Vice and Immorality (its later name) became the subject of several Parliamentary debates. But by that time, the old order had not only realised its danger, but was already fighting a rearguard action. At the time, it seems clear that only a few zealots took the matter seriously at all.

Wilberforce himself expected no spectacular results, though he evidently did expect some action.

> I know that by regulating external conduct we do not change the hearts of men [he wrote to a friend], but even they are ultimately wrought upon by these means, and we should at least so far remove the obtrusiveness of temptation that it may not provoke the appetite which might otherwise be dormant and inactive.

It is the reverse of the Freudian method of reformation, working from the surface inward instead of from the centre outward. But, on the whole and in the long run, it succeeded. At the same time, one can perhaps detect in it the seed which gave rise to the crop of Stigginses and Pecksniffs in the next generation.

The peculiar insistence on the observation of Sunday was of the greatest importance in the campaign. Other items in the Society's programme were defensible from a rational point of view—that is, defensible as being desirable, not necessarily as suitable to be enforced by law. Drunkenness and gambling to excess can be attacked by any thinking person. Swearing is not a polite or pretty habit. Even the irreligious may disap-

prove of sexual promiscuity and of obscene publications. But the only reason for observing Sunday
rigorously is that it is so commanded in the Bible. By
this emphasis the reformers marked themselves off as
rebels to the rule of Reason. The observance of Sunday
became their badge. Mrs. Trimmer, who served as one
of the most useful non-commissioned officers in the
campaign, expressed this directly. The observance of
Sunday, she said, 'brought with it a peculiar blessing,
as the *sign* which was to distinguish the servants of the
Lord and mark them as his people'.

Naturally, this insistence on an irrelevant and irra-
tional practice (from any but the strict Christian point
of view) aroused more impatience and antagonism in
the easy-going society of the time than any attempt to
reform morals. One might have expected that Wilberforce and his friends would have had more chance of
success—and in 1787 and for many years afterwards
their crusade must have appeared a forlorn hope—if
they had not thrown such emphasis on this point.
Actually, in sharply cutting off the sheep from the
goats, it gave the movement force and purity: it
excluded all lukewarm Christians and secular moralists. The members of the open conspiracy had to be
earnest in their piety, to accept the bible literally, to
believe in original sin and to see human life solemnly
as merely the preparation for an eternity which was
all-important. When Wilberforce tried to prevent the
training of the militia on Sundays, it was because he
thought it less important that England should not be
conquered by the French than that the word of God
should be obeyed.* For the same reason he would not

* Alternatively, he sometimes used the argument that the
French menace was probably God's punishment for disobedience
and therefore the stopping of the training would be the best
defence.

17

have Parliament recalled on a Monday, however desperate the situation, because that would oblige members to travel on Sunday. His criticism of Swift is unique—'What a thoroughly irreligious mind—no trace of Sunday to be found in his Journals or letters to his most intimate friends!' Even Castlereagh's suicide he attributed to non-observance of Sunday, though, in this instance, resurgent rationality seems to have demanded a little hedging. Wilberforce explains that a change of occupation on Sundays would have relaxed the tension of the statesman's mind.

Of the same nature was the attack on the theatre, though, as there was no law against this, except for Sunday performances, it could not be inserted in the Proclamation. Nor is any such prohibition to be found in the Scriptures. This may, of course, be because at the time and place of writing, there were no theatres to be banned; but no one could prove that they would have been banned if they had existed. Yet a person who is to be constantly preoccupied with ideas of sin, death and judgment should obviously avoid all vivid distractions which might divert his attention from his predicament. 'The amusements of a Christian', wrote Hannah More, 'must have nothing in them to excite the passions which it is his duty to subdue; they must not obstruct spiritual-mindedness, nor inflame "the lust of the flesh, lust of the eye and pride of life".' The more he appreciates the theatre, the more the Christian should deny himself the gratification. Good plays are even more dangerous to good people than are bad ones.*

* Yet the same author says elsewhere that 'intoxication affords no just reason against the use of wine'. It seems curious that there was no ['Total Abstinence' movement among the early Evangelicals; that came in mid-Victorian times. Possibly, water supplies were then too unreliable for abstinence from wine to seem feasible.

The writer of this passage knew what she was talking about. Like Wilberforce, she had had a cheerful youth and enjoyed the best that eighteenth-century society could give. To neither of them could anyone use the 'sour grapes' taunt. Indeed, to be a successful playwright would seem to many an even higher point of felicity than to be an eloquent young M.P. in the Prime Minister's counsels. And yet she, too, renounced the worldly life, and her former position ensured that her new stand should have hardly less effect than Wilberforce's. Though they did not meet until several years later, their conversions were almost simultaneous.

Hannah More was another infiltrator from the middle classes into the upper. Though Society was aristocratic, such infiltration was then easy and frequent —the very broad-mindedness of the social arbiters made it so. Entry was open to wealth, if accompanied by a certain minimum of polish, to talent and to anyone who knew how to be entertaining.

Hannah More brought a sufficiency of all these qualifications, though she never had such a fortune as Wilberforce's. Her father was a Bristol schoolmaster, with a family of five daughters, all of whom remained unmarried and all of whom were energetic, with intellectual tastes. Hannah was the most expressive of the five. She was educated by her father, who, however, refused to teach her Latin and Mathematics, lest he should rear a female pedant. In view of his daughter's later career, this seems unfortunate. Study of the classics might have given her a wider and more mellow culture; a mathematical training might have reduced her voluminous works to greater concision and exactness.

Her start to fame and fortune is a curious story, which she had to some extent to live down. She had been engaged to a rich elderly Bristol merchant who, for some reason, successfully concealed from the public, kept postponing the marriage. Ultimately, he offered her an annuity, which, after much taking of advice and consultation with friends, she found herself able to accept; and, when he died, he left her a legacy of £1,000, a considerable sum for a single, middle-class woman in those days.

Like most ambitious young English people of all times—she was still not quite thirty—Hannah made straight for London. Being already the author of some verse and a published play for children, she was there adopted by the Blue-Stocking circle and the allied one of Johnson, Reynolds and Burke.

These 'blue-stocking' women'* formed a serious-minded wing of cultured society in the latter half of the eighteenth century. From one point of view, they played the part of a Trojan Horse in the citadel of High Civilisation. They were the champions of their sex in winning their way into the sphere of intellectual tastes and interests; but, at the same time, they introduced a solid wedge of feminine conservatism, respect for convention (apart from the particular one they were attacking) and a certain ineradicable earnestness, in spite of all their wit and charm. The fashion that women in Society should be highly educated had come from the French *salons*; but, in the French *salons*, refined taste, wide scholarship, and brilliant conversation were combined with adventure and experiment in the Art of Love. Any educated Frenchman or Frenchwoman would have been shocked at the idea that they should not be. Here, the English Blue-Stockings could not follow. On the contrary they set great store by propriety—a word they constantly used. Hannah More herself wrote of the unfortunate Mrs.

* The term 'blue-stocking' was not at first exclusively used of women, though it soon became so.

Macauley, who had married a man much younger than herself, that she had never esteemed her, and how provoking it was that the men were exulting at her downfall! But 'she was not feminine—only a tolerably clever man!'—a curious conclusion. Again Miss Carter, the Greek scholar, writing to Mrs. Montagu in 1788, was shocked at the custom of inviting lovers to parties with their mistresses. 'A species of corruption', she says, 'which must make every sober mind shudder' and, she adds, 'inconsistent with the Spirit of the Gospel'.

Again, the final phrase seems a trifle incongruous. Religious allusions are not common in the writings of the Blue-Stockings; in contrast to the next generation of educated women, they say little on such subjects, though what they do say is almost as conventionally pious. French agnosticism was as little to their taste as French free love. Their superiority and emancipation were expressed rather as contempt for the frequenters of card parties and gambling clubs, for female gossip and tattle and intrigue, and for all who did not understand the higher pleasures of intellectual conversation and the charm of the *salons*.

But it was a real charm, in spite of the limitations of 'propriety'. Boswell describes one occasion—a little party of choice spirits which marked the return of Mrs. Garrick to society after her long mourning for her husband's death. It took place at her home in the Adelphi and the guests were Mrs. Boscawen, Miss Carter and Hannah More from the Blue-Stocking circles, Dr. Johnson, Sir Joshua Reynolds, Dr. Burney and Boswell. The spirit of Garrick, 'who gladdened life', seemed to preside encouragingly over the gathering of his friends from his portrait over the chimney-piece. Dr. Johnson was in an amiable mood and there was good conversation, good food and special toasts

in Lichfield ale. All were in fine spirits. Boswell failed
to record much of the conversation, though the general
effect of the day, he said, dwelt in his mind 'in fond
rememberance'. They talked about books, about
Johnson's 'candour' in criticism, the question whether
a literary life might be as entertaining as a life of
action, about odd personalities and queer happenings.
One ominous lapse into vulgarity occurred when Hannah hid her face on Johnson's remarking that some
woman 'had a bottom of common-sense'; but Johnson
marched over her. More distinguished and congenial
guests came in the evening. Boswell calls it one of the
happiest days he remembered to have enjoyed. 'I
whispered to Mrs. Boscawen, "I believe that this is
as much as can be made of life."'

One would hesitate to claim Boswell as the typical
civilised man of the eighteenth century, but he expressed for it there an essential value, unsuspecting
that the iconoclast, the future renegade from human
'sweetness and light', was actually present as he said it.

The connection of the Blue-Stockings with Dr.
Johnson, one of the most deeply religious men of his
irreligious generation, naturally encouraged their bias
towards virtue. But, even in him, there was none of the
pious absorption of the next generation. In fact, he
was long and painfully discussed by Hannah More's
biographer in 1855, to ascertain whether he might be
considered to have been converted on his death-bed to
a 'better understanding of the Christian atonement'.

Except for Fanny Burney, Hannah More was the
youngest recruit of the Blue-Stockings. The original
pioneers—they never had any formal constitution—
were all in later middle-age by the time she reached
London and their glory lasted only a few years longer.
She celebrated it before it was too late in her poem the
'Bas Bleu', still gaily unaware that it was she herself

who was to give a new and less lively turn to female intellect and energy.

Hannah More's conversion, unlike Wilberforce's, seems to have been a gradual process. Her family must have been more religious than his,* for the 'Sabbath' idea was present in her from the first. One of her letters home of 1775 apologises for having gone to a party on Sunday. But she repeated the lapse a week later and felt unrepentant, because it was not 'in trifling company', i.e. it was with the Blue-Stockings, where the conversation was 'sprightly but serious'. She never played cards, in spite of ridicule. A natural distaste for large social functions seems to have assisted her progress towards serious-mindedness. She said she disliked them all, except plays, and even those she would be content to abandon when Garrick went.

It was an embarrassment to her nineteenth century biographer that Hannah More not merely formed a warm friendship with Garrick and his wife, but wrote plays herself—though always tragedies—during her years in London. He defends himself for recording 'the light and unspiritual intercourse' of those days by the necessity of showing what trials and temptations she had to overcome. The moral is a little spoilt by the fact that the temptation was not overcome until it was largely removed by Garrick's retirement and death soon afterwards. Yet Hannah herself found it necessary to defend her dead friend—and, perhaps, also herself—to a correspondent by praising the 'decorum and propriety' of his mode of life. She never, she says, saw a card in his house, nor (a curious tribute, to the

* Probably because his was a wealthy commercial family and hers a scholastic, rather than by reason of any greater piety in Bristol than in Hull. The general opinion at the time was that irreligion and dissipation were much more rife in the South than in the North.

modern mind) met there, except once, another member of his own profession.

But even more disconcerting to her later admirers, than her success as a playwright or her association with Garrick, was Hannah's much longer friendship with Horace Walpole. It lasted, in fact, until his death in 1797, long after she had left London, absorbed herself in good works and become so immersed in her religion that she could not bear to hear the phrases, 'The Christening of a Ship', the 'Salvation of a Country', 'Trinity Lane' or the 'Ascension of a Balloon'; long after she had been dubbed by Walpole himself 'Saint Hannah'. It seems an amiable trait in the pious woman that she should never have dropped her correspondence with this frivolous, but now ageing worldling. But her biographer agonises in his apologies for it, falling back at last on the dictum that perfect consistency is found only in Heaven. Anyhow, he adds, rallying, she would certainly have dropped Walpole if he had lived a few years longer 'in her own advance in spirituality'.

Garrick died in 1779. In the next few years Hannah More gradually relinquished even the refined and mitigated social life she had hitherto allowed herself. By 1783, she could say she had long withdrawn from the theatre and that she did not go to any of the six or eight dinners and assemblies to which she was invited in one week. One lady, whose Sunday assembly she refused, though she never had cards, only 'a little agreeable music', called her a 'savage and rigid Methodist'.

Johnson followed Garrick in 1784; and the Blue-Stocking ladies, one may presume, were not what they had been. Mrs. Thrale had seceded on her misalliance, Fanny Burney had been rapt away into the royal household; all the *prima donnas* of the circle were now in their sixties. It is likely that the invitations, accepted or not, became fewer. Hannah decided to leave London and retire to a country cottage, which move she hoped would 'favour her escape from the world gradually'.

Apart from this geographical translation, there was nothing abrupt or dramatic about Hannah More's adoption of the religious life, and it is more easily to be understood by the uninitiated than Wilberforce's conversion. They took their respective drastic steps within a few months of each other, but, whereas he was a young man of twenty-seven in the full tide of success, she was a woman of forty who had had her 'good time' and enjoyed all she wanted of society. A retirement in good order was probably desirable as much from common-sense motives, as from religious ones. Nor was it by any means complete. For many years, she spent most of the spring and early summer in London with Mrs. Garrick and she paid frequent visits in other parts of the country.

'She now', says her biographer of 1834, advancing with renewed strength on to more congenial ground, 'began to dedicate her powerful talents to the more immediate service of God and the benefit of his rational creatures.' In other words, she felt, like Wilberforce, the need of a manifesto. She had begun to fear, she says, that her London associates thought that her views agreed with theirs, since all that one could do in Society was to point out truths on common subjects and express sentiments drawn from religion—it was all that they would endure. 'Fine people' would indeed join in reprobating vice, 'for they are not *all* vicious . . . but their standard of life is low, it is not the standard of the Gospel'.

The Proclamation of 1787 gave an opportunity for her to make her avowal, and it seems something of an anticlimax that this avowal, which took the form of a book, *Thoughts on the Importance of the Manners of the Great to General Society*, should, after all, have been published anonymously. But one can sympathise with her timidity. Wilberforce had been braver, but even he had shrunk from stepping out before that critical audience in his new rôle. Moreover, it was common at the time for women writers to publish anonymously, though the identity of the author usually leaked out very quickly if the book had any success. Hannah herself gave two reasons for concealing her name, a rational, if somewhat equivocal one, that, as her principles were loftier than her practice, she hoped the book would be attributed to some better person; and one more naive, that she was afraid of being ostracised if she were known to be the author. In her case, too, the truth soon leaked out; but she went on publishing anonymously, up to her four last books. In fact, her anonymity became a standing joke and finally an irritation to her friends, since, before long, any practised reader could recognise her work at sight.

Her fears proved quite unfounded. As usual, Society did not in the least mind having its sins pointed out. And, after all, the attack was not on the more lurid sins, but mainly on 'the good sort of man', with a respectable reputation, which would, however, as the author insists, stand him in little stead on the Day of Judgment. Her intention was to supplement the King's Proclamation by listing minor offences which were generally condoned. Various forms of Sabbath-breaking are inevitably the most numerous. Then there was the lie of 'not at home', so demoralising to servants,* and the false identification of extravagance with generosity, with a look askance at Charles Sur-

* However, Wilberforce's servants found the reverse policy extremely inconvenient; and so did he.

face in *The School for Scandal*, and that 'alarming symptom', that the distinctions of right and wrong were almost swept away in polite conversation; for instance, the use of the word 'gallantry' to cover adultery. Hannah More does not use this last term; she calls it 'that crime which stabs domestic happiness and conjugal virtue'.

One suspects that Society must have been a little disappointed at the mildness of the attack, especially as everything is put in general terms, with no suggestion of personalities. They might well have shunned the book for its tediousness rather than execrated it for its offensiveness. But they did neither. A few protested gently that the author's idea of Sunday observance was too rigid, Horace Walpole pointing out that Sunday was made for the poor; fashionable people didn't need it. But the book went into four editions within the year and many more later. In the twentieth century it is almost unreadable.

At the time that Hannah More left London, she and Wilberforce had never met. But they had a mentor in common, the Newton who had received Wilberforce's first confidences about his conversion. Not long after this, this evangelist was writing long letters of advice and exhortation to Hannah, who found, to her chagrin, that she was not improving herself in leisure and solitude as she had expected, and was told that she was relying too much on her own strength. The two converts met in 1788 at Bath, where everyone who was anyone went sooner or later.*

---

* Bath waters were the fashionable cure-all at the time. Many people persuaded their doctors to send them there, but Wilberforce and Hannah More were genuine cases. The invalidism of both was only just short of chronic. Yet they must both have been fundamentally tough, since Wilberforce died at seventy-four and Hannah More at eighty-eight. She said she had survived fifteen doctors who had attended her.

Wilberforce's first comment on Hannah 'a most excellent woman' seems a little cold, but no doubt meant a great deal from him. Hers on him is more enthusiastic. 'That young gentleman's character is one of the most extraordinary I ever knew for talents, virtue and piety. It is difficult not to grow wiser and better every time one converses with him.' Later, he became, for her, 'the Red-Cross Knight'. The meeting naturally led to a life-long friendship and partnership in the moral crusade. For Hannah soon found something else to do besides her literary attacks on the sins of Society, and it was Wilberforce who switched her energies in the new direction. When on a visit to her, he was so shocked at the neglected condition of the people of Cheddar, particularly at their spiritual neglect by a non-resident vicar and a curate who came only on Sundays, that he decided something must be done, and told his hostess, 'If you will be at the trouble, I will be at the expense.'

This was the beginning of the well-known pioneering effort of Hannah and her sisters in providing education for the poor. Sunday schools had been started some years before by Raikes, but someone of larger influence in a wider society was necessary to popularise the movement. Hannah's effort encountered all manner of obstacles, many of them due to the overwhelming emphasis she laid on religious instruction. The farmers objected that religion would make their labourers idle and useless. Mothers wanted to be paid for sending their children to school; some refused because their notion of the law was that, after seven years, the teacher would acquire rights in the children and might send them overseas. Churchmen, clerics and lay, of the usual easy views, accused her of Methodism. She was summoned before the Dean's Court under an obsolete law that a schoolmaster must have a licence. A drunken farmer invaded the school in session. When, later, the fear of French Revolutionary doctrines became acute, opposition to any education for the working-classes increased. Hannah herself was affected by it. She wrote to the Bishop of Bath and Wells that she taught on weekdays only 'such coarse works as may fit them for servants . . . no writing for the poor, only habits of industry and piety'. 'I do not vindicate enthusiasm, I dread it,' she assured him.

In spite of all obstruction, the experiment was a great success. It expanded into women's clubs, religious services for adults, technical training for young women in spinning, etc. It also spread geographically to surrounding districts. But the predominant element was always religion. 'One mere child,' remarked Wilberforce joyfully in 1792, 'had brought all his father's household to family prayers.' The impulse spread further. Religious and energetic women everywhere began to imitate her. Wilberforce, perhaps, inadvertently put his finger on the motive force behind the movement when he remarked in later years, discussing Hannah More's work, 'There is no class of persons whose condition has been more improved in my experience than that of unmarried women. Formerly there seemed to be nothing useful in which they could naturally be busy, but now they may always find an object in attending the poor.'

What the Blue-Stocking ladies had done for the release of intelligent women of the upper classes, their younger apprentice, with very different ends in view, was now doing for the women of the lesser gentry and the middle classes, who, in those days, when to have only one or two servants was the depth of genteel poverty, had been confined to needlework, gossip, amateur music and painting and husband-hunting.

Young Mary Butt (the future Mrs. Sherwood, author of *The Fairchild Family*) and her sister, taken into unduly sordid retirement at Bridgnorth by their widowed mother in 1796, were of those who found this new outlet. A Mrs. King, an intimate of Hannah More, who went about organising schools and other social welfare schemes, put them on the track and they took to teaching in Sunday schools, distributing tracts and prescribing medicines. Though Mary and her sister reverted gladly to more frivolous pursuits when the chance came, she records, 'That little peep into the religious world which I then had opened a perfectly new scene to me,' and, as with Wilberforce, it returned upon her later.

Meanwhile, Hannah herself was becoming a very different woman from the playwright and wit of the salons. Wilberforce was now to her what Garrick had been in the early years. When her best and most successful play, *Percy*, was revived with Mrs. Siddons as the heroine she would not go to it, although she was in London at the time. Hand and brain became subdued to what they worked in. By 1793, she could say, 'I should derive more gratification from being able to lower the price of bread than from having written the *Iliad*.' This sentiment recalls—by contrast—Wolfe's remark that he would rather have written Gray's *Elegy* than take Quebec. Certainly, in our twentieth-century climate of opinion, to lower the price of bread would be a high, almost a sacred achievement, far higher than the taking of Quebec or any other city. But the *Iliad*! It might make a good test question for dividing the civilised from the decivilised.

* II *
OPEN CONSPIRACY

Things are coming to a pretty pass when religion is allowed to invade private life.

LORD MELBOURNE

THE two illustrious converts described in the last chapter had so powerful an effect in the purification—and the narrowing—of English social life that it seems doubtful whether even the French Revolution, the Industrial Revolution and the Napoleonic wars could, without them, have produced a change recognisably like that which occurred. The question brings up the old controversy whether the course of History is determined by great individuals or by a blind social evolution. Fortunately, it is not necessary to choose between the two theories, though many historians appear to feel that they must do so. In the same way, the course of an individual life is apt to be attributed either entirely to the character of the individual or to external chances. Yet every adult, looking back, knows well enough that both these influences have been at work in varying proportions in his own life, that either may be decisive at some particular moment and that the result is an unanalysable combination of the two. So it is with personalities and social trends in the lifetime of a society. One must be content with dual, or even multiple causes. Wilberforce's conversion and Hannah More's were both highly individual performances, owing nothing to the French Revolution, which had not yet happened. But whether they could have produced any such profound effect as they did without it equally remains an open question.

31

It was not merely a matter of their own work and their personal influence, important as these were. Their recruitment gave a lift to a number of comparatively obscure workers for religious and moral reform. Methodism, with its evangelical reaction in the Church, was a movement coming from below, and the earlier converts, except for a few recognised eccentrics, were not of the classes that set the tone of Society. But henceforth these underminers had their active agents in the political and the fashionable world and among the intellectuals. The gain in prestige was enormous.

The more vigorous and intelligent of the pioneers now began to form a close network of inter-relations and to co-ordinate their efforts more and more. Wilberforce and Hannah More had been linked through Newton, and soon after had their fruitful meeting. Newton was linked with the poet Cowper, whose physical and mental frailty prevented him from taking any practical part in the campaign, but who was quite capable of telling literary attacks on the vices of the age.

A sturdier contributor was the formidable Mrs. Trimmer, whom Hannah More had met even before she left London. Mrs. Trimmer had expounded Raikes's ideas on Sunday Schools in a book called *The Oeconomy of Charity*. She was one of the first of the busy, bustling, socially-minded Christian women who became so numerous in the next generation. As with Hannah More, Sunday schools were for her the nucleus of many other activities. Brentford, where she lived, showed a visible change in manners in consequence of her labours, as Hannah reported. But at this time Mrs. Trimmer's effect was only local; though she was well off and of good connections, she had nothing approaching Hannah's social influence. Later, she was to carry the campaign for serious-mindedness into other fields; and from her family went forth the missionary who penetrated the utmost stronghold of High Society. At this early date, the Bishop of Salisbury remarked that Hannah More wanted to reform the Great, and Mrs. Trimmer the Poor, adding that he thought the latter enterprise the more hopeful. But each of the two good women encroached on the other's domain in course of time.

Lady Spencer was another London friend of Hannah More. She also knew Mrs. Trimmer and may well have sponsored their first meeting. She herself had the hard fate—for a woman of austere religious principles —of being the mother of the famous Duchess of Devonshire, and of Lady Bessborough. She was of middle-class origin, 'the daughter', as Horace Walpole put it, 'of a nobleman's tutor'. This was hardly fair, since 'the nobleman's tutor' had risen through his own ability to high diplomatic posts and had become a Privy Councillor. But Lady Spencer had probably had a conventionally religious background, though even she was said to have been fond of the gaming-tables in her youth.

The conflict between Lady Spencer and her brilliant, impulsive, free-living daughters was never resolved. They always respected, and deceived her when they could; and sometimes, after all, went to her for help and advice in their more desperate scrapes. She maintained her stand all her life. It was through her that Selina Trimmer,* whose mission work in High Society will be described in the next chapter, was introduced as governess into Devonshire House.

* Virginia Woolf in her essay in *The Captain's Death-Bed*, makes Selina, Mrs. Trimmer's sister-in-law, not her daughter, and she is so described in a footnote in *Letters of Harriet, Countess Granville*; but the evidence on the other side is overwhelming.

All these pioneers of reformation seem to have been acquainted with the Bowdlers, a family prolific in pious literature, whose ultimate achievement in the purged edition of Shakespeare has contributed a word to the English language.

The Clergy among this group were paradoxically something of outcasts in their own profession in these early days. They were suspect for 'enthusiasm'. Charles Simeon, in what later proved to be a key position at Cambridge, had his Sunday evening services turned into undergraduate rags, because it was considered 'Methodistical' to hold evening services at all. Wilberforce's sons and biographers (both themselves clergymen) were bitter in their own more propitious times, about 'the lukewarmness and apathy which possessed the very watchmen of the faith' at the time of their father's conversion. This they attributed to 'the deadly leaven of Hoadly's Latitudinarian views', and these views had indeed been useful to those clergymen—naturally very numerous in the eighteenth century—who wanted their share in the cultured pleasant life of the man of the world. Wilberforce himself describes one such—'the true picture of a sensible, well-informed and educated, polished, old, well-beneficed, nobleman's and gentleman's house-frequenting, literary and chess-playing divine'. These good days were now approaching their end. Wilberforce, with his strategic eye, at once seized upon the reform of the clergy as a major objective in his campaign. He had rounded up many of the bishops by means of the Proclamation of 1787. Both of the Archbishops and seventeen other bishops signed the Prospectus of the Proclamation Society, though it is notable that only one of them was on the Committee. But their adherence, whether eager or reluctant, strengthened the position of the Newtons and the

Milners in the Church, and weakened that of the 'buck parsons' like the one who stipulated for a sporting country and a convivial neighbourhood. This gentleman, at least, evidently intended to live in his cure; at the time, it was extremely common for one man to hold several livings and perhaps rarely visit any one of them. The execrated Hoadly had set the example by never visiting his diocese when he was Bishop of Bangor. Underpaid, overworked curates (though there were evidently another sort, too) did whatever duties could not be shirked. Hannah More had found that, in Cheddar, children were often buried without Christian rites.

The reformers set their faces against clerical absenteeism. A Yorkshire clergyman who, very much mistaking his man, approached Wilberforce to help him to obtain a dispensation for non-residence because he had been used to live in literary circles in London and could not endure the dearth of intellectual society in the country, had Hannah More quoted to him as an example. The practice, however, was very slow to disappear or even diminish; it was too convenient for younger sons and other protégés of the aristocracy, who must be provided for somehow, but had no desire or intention to live in the country. As late as 1814, Jane Austen, to whom one does not usually go for the discussion of sociological problems, made the plot of *Mansfield Park* turn on this question; and, though she is firmly on the side of dutifulness, it is clear that many people still were not, and that the Clergy Residence Act of 1810 was still liberally interpreted. In *Northanger Abbey*, drafted some fifteen years earlier, the hero incurs no unfavourable comment in visiting his parish only at weekends and on other occasional days. Bishop Blomfield in the see of Chester in 1824 was still fighting against non-resident clergy.

This branch of the campaign had to be slow. In fact, it was practically a question of waiting for the older generation to die and then, so far as might be, bringing in evangelical successors. Hannah More suffered helpless indignation when a local curate was dismissed for 'Methodism' after preaching against the theatre, and his rector showed what he thought of it by treating forty 'poor wretches' (as Hannah calls them) among the parishioners to a shilling play. And even when such rectors died, it was no easy matter to introduce 'real Christians' in their place. Most livings were in the gift of magnates great and small who had their own ideas and not often predominantly spiritual ones. But Wilberforce educated many chosen theological students at his own expense and helped to find them livings.* He was also in a position to influence higher ecclesiastical appointments—it was through him that Milner became Dean of Carlisle—and so to bring pressure to bear on the rank and file of the clergy. In this way, the profession gradually became less attractive to those who were not prepared to take it seriously.

However, from the first, the reformers found one outstanding champion among the bishops. One of those whom Wilberforce had intended to visit and canvass for his Proclamation Society in the summer of 1787 was Bishop Porteus of Chester; but he was saved the long journey by meeting a messenger on the road carrying the bishop's enthusiastic assent. In the same year, Porteus was translated from the see of Chester to that of London and, if George III realised what he was doing in making this appointment, he, too, must

* At a later stage, when they had become much stronger, the reformers took to buying up presentations to small livings where the population was increasing, and putting in their own men. But this is spoken of as still a new problem in Bishop Butler's Correspondence in 1835.

be regarded as one of the major conspirators in the overthrow of the eighteenth century manner of life.

There was no 'lukewarm Christianity' about Bishop Porteus. In his opinion the very existence of Christianity in England depended upon observance of the Lord's Day. He had already carried through an act against the Promenades on Sundays at Carlisle House, and against Sunday debating societies, which were supposed to be for the discussion of religious subjects, but, actually, according to him, had become a forum for rationalists and sceptics. The bishop seems to have been something of a spiritual swashbuckler, to whom his nineteenth-century biographer did more—or less —than justice, in a 'Life' of the expanded epitaph type. He was always making spectacular dashes against the frivolities of High Society, especially when they infringed on the Sabbath. He was constantly involving himself or the Proclamation Society, of which he was the third president, in all kinds of law cases, including many against the sale of such immoral books as Tom Paine's *Age of Reason*. He waged war against clerical absenteeism until common informers made such a nuisance of themselves that something had to be done to check them in 1802. In his official position, he could not have the pervasive social influence that Wilberforce and Hannah More exercised, but he could be and was of immense use to them and their friends. Fulham Palace became a headquarters of the open conspiracy in the heart of the enemy's country. Hannah More often stayed there, helping to plan new sallies against her old friends, and the bishop was believed largely to have directed her literary output.

Such was the disposal of the forces of the new Puritanism when the shock which had been preparing in France broke upon the society whose standards they were undermining from within. This shock did not follow immediately on the fall of the Bastille in 1789. Englishmen were inclined to approve of the French Revolution in its early phases, supposing it to be a belated imitation of their own revolution of 1688. It was not until the Terror of 1793 and the outbreak of war that they began to be dismayed.

The reformers did not, of course, recognise the general scare, passing into a long-drawn strain and consciousness of danger, as the ally that it proved to be. Wilberforce, as a politician, was always working for peace, and he never lost the idea that the war had hindered his moral campaign and that British society would have improved far more rapidly if it had not occurred. This belief indeed clashed with his other view that the war was God's punishment for the country's iniquities, since a punishment that makes the culprit worse can hardly be said to answer its purpose. But Wilberforce was never a theologian. Perhaps the fact that the war certainly hindered his other campaign for the abolition of the Slave Trade affected his outlook. Not only this, but every other progressive measure was held up indefinitely by it. With the fear of a Fifth Column in their midst, people naturally veered to Conservatism; they wanted no change in established institutions; and Abolitionists, along with Methodists and 'enthusiasts' generally, were lumped with revolutionaries. On the other hand, the general need for comfort and reassurance brought many flocking back to Church and to the religious standards they had deserted. Moral reform thus flourished at the expense of political.

At the same time, it is easy in our own days to overestimate the effect of the war on society at home in England. It was never a 'total war' as the twentieth century knows it. Invasion seemed imminent from time to time, but no bombs dropped; the press-gang rounded up derelicts, but there was no conscription. Local defence arrangements were mainly voluntary. Women were not involved except by rising prices and in the anxiety of those who had relatives and friends in the forces; and these were always a minority. Times were harder, but the pattern of life was not vitally altered, especially for the upper classes.

When Wilberforce plunged into authorship on behalf of his principles in 1797, he made no mention of the war and only a couple of indirect, almost casual, allusions to it. But it may not be quite irrelevant to the book's success that, at that moment, Britain had, as usual, lost all the opening campaigns, except at sea, and all her allies, and that the National Debt was mounting at what then seemed an appalling rate. An attitude of gay insouciance must have become less easy to maintain.

Wilberforce's manifesto, to give it its full title, was *A Practical View of the Prevailing Religious System of Professed Christians in the Higher and Middle Classes in this Country Contrasted with Real Christianity*. Though the literary digestion of our ancestors was certainly stronger than our own, it was no doubt fortunate for the book's circulation that the first and last words could be taken to form a more manageable title, *Practical Christianity*. It posed once more the crucial question, 'If you believe this, why do you not behave accordingly?'

'This present scene,' says the Introduction, 'with all its cares and all its gaieties, will soon be rolled away, and we must stand before the judgment seat of Christ! This awful consideration will prompt the writer to express himself with greater freedom than he should otherwise be disposed to use.' This slightly ludicrous apology to old standards of urbanity, with its suggestion that the universe might have been 'otherwise' than he conceived it to be, was perhaps a final farewell to the tolerant young Wilberforce of the early eighties. He was now summoning his countrymen to a similar farewell. They must abandon their 'rational religion', which in practice meant 'lukewarm', and their lives of 'decent selfishness'. Even those whose ideal was 'amiable tempers and useful lives' were superficial, could not stand up against hard knocks and often used their principles merely as an excuse for officiousness. And, for most, pleasure was the great business of life. There follow attacks on the abuse of the Sabbath, on duelling and on the love of fame in all its forms.

The bookseller had told the author that there was little demand for religious publications and had budgeted for 500 copies. In fact, 7,500 were sold in six months and, by 1826, there had been fifteen editions. Wilberforce's sons claim that 'it may be affirmed beyond all question that it gave the first general impulse to that warmer and more earnest burst of piety which, among all its many evils, has happily distinguished the last half century'.

Wilberforce married in the same year and the comment made on this—that he showed his confidence in God by deciding to marry at such a time—suggests how badly the confidence of the country had been shaken. Actually, he had offered to release his future wife from the engagement on the news of the Naval mutiny at the Nore, because he thought his life might be in danger if the French seized the opportunity to invade.

Since several instances of direct conversion through *Practical Christianity* are recorded, it may be supposed that there were many others. Arthur Young, the agriculturalist, who argued with the Unitarian Duke of Grafton, was one. Wilberforce himself mentions, among others, a Mr. Richmond who 'became serious through reading my book on Christianity'. Others, like Eliot, Pitt's brother-in-law, were converted through personal loss or misfortune, and this motive naturally operated more frequently in war-time. Mary Butt's gay young life was again interrupted; she and her sister were made 'more serious' by hearing of the deaths of young men with whom they had danced. They gave up pleasures and society to a great extent and others did the same. Financial losses due to the war kept some families in the country who had been accustomed to a London Season every year. There, the practice of family prayers, which even Wilberforce had found embarrassing when he first tried it, began to spread.

The frequent recurrence of the word 'serious' in the reformers' writings is symptomatic. The word was becoming specialised to mean 'religious'; but religion was meeting it half-way. Wilberforce had told Pitt that his religion would not be gloomy; and he answered a critic in the House by the crushing remark 'that a religious man may sometimes be facetious' while 'the irreligious did not of necessity escape being dull'. But this sparkle was followed by repentance; the next day he was reproaching himself for having lacked 'unruffled love' and for 'fermentation of spirits'. In the same way, Hannah More, after writing a satirical review of a novel by someone who had dared to attack Garrick, determined that she would never indulge in 'sarcastic humour' again. Since it is difficult to be amusing without sometimes treading on people's toes, this self-denial had a far from enlivening effect on the literary—and, one may suppose, conversational—style of both. Wilberforce's filial biographers constantly emphasise the gaiety and wit of his conversation; but it is baffling that they give hardly any instances, though this may, of course, be more symptomatic of their own bias than of their father's. He seems, in any case, to have broken out occasionally. Madame de Stael, having insisted on meeting him in 1814, very much against his will, remarked that she had heard he was the most religious and now found that he was the wittiest man in England. But, again, the result for Wilberforce was two pages of self-reproach in his diary the next day. 'The fever of it is not yet gone off (half-past eight a.m.) though opposed by the most serious motives and considerations last night and this morning. I am sure I durst not often venture into these scenes.'

In the early days Wilberforce had solemnly consulted Hannah More as to whether he ought to suppress his natural gaiety in society. She advised him to use this gift to further religion and to gain something upon the frivolous. One can only come to the conclusion that the odds were too heavy. Hannah had been witty herself in her youth as the '*Blas Bleu*' bears witness; but her later work, like that of other pious writers of the time, almost drives one to the conclusion that there is some correlation between religious zeal and garrulity. That she did not bore her contemporaries, or at least not the greater part of them, is, for a modern reader, an illustration of the vital difficulty of entering into the mental attitude of another age.

Religious conversion, however, inevitably involves transvaluation, and one can see the point of Wilberforce's comment on Sheridan: 'He seems to live on that, to me, melancholy distich, Life is a jest etc.' * Among the reformers, as their campaign proceeded, a great part of their correspondence was taken up by accounts of 'triumphant' death-beds. One can see it

* No doubt, the well-known epitaph:
   'Life is a jest and all things show it,
   I thought so once and now I know it.'

developing almost into a competition. In one sense, this may be regarded as a more cheerful attitude than that of Sheridan. But it did not make for wit or charm; nor for a good literary style.

The reformers sometimes went to surprising lengths in these religious reversals of natural sentiments—surprising, that is, in a faction that remained within what Brougham called that 'quiet and somewhat lazy Church', the Anglican Establishment, and came, for a time, almost to dominate it. Wilberforce's condolences with one of his friends on the early death of a daughter almost approached congratulation. No doubt, he said, she had gone in a state of grace, but would she always have remained so? 'I can imagine that Lady Maria would have had several serious obstacles to her religious advancement to contend with.' Most people who have suffered bereavement have at times to endure well-meaning, but obtuse efforts at consolation from the narrowly pious; but it must have required a very tough Christian to take such a suggestion in perfectly good part. But Wilberforce was capable of an equally uncompromising attitude to his own ailing daughter. 'May her ill-health be blessed to her,' he wrote, 'and then it may be, nay, will be matter for rejoicing.' Only a little less severe is Hannah More's farewell to friends leaving the country, 'My wishes and prayers will attend you both that you may enjoy health, prosperity and all earthly comforts, as far as they may be good for your eternal interests.' 'Serious' people had always an eye on these eternal interests and, as this type of seriousness became fashionable, this way of talking spread even to those who cannot be suspected of deep feeling on the subject.

In the last few years of the eighteenth century, after the publication of *Practical Christianity*, the assault of

43

the serious on the frivolous worked up to a crescendo. The battle for the Sabbath was always the fiercest. At this time, Wilberforce succeeded in preventing the training of the Militia on Sundays against Pitt's natural reluctance. But he and his friends lost a bill to stop the sale of Sunday newspapers in the face of the 'gibes' of Sheridan, who pointed out that Sunday newspapers were, in fact, printed on Saturdays, while Sunday was the only day on which many people could give any attention to public affairs. Mackerel, he said, was permitted to be sold on Sundays, and was not stale news as bad as stale mackerel?

Fashionable society was now becoming a little more aware of what was going on. The Proclamation Society was forced also to abandon a bill against Sunday amusements, but substituted a declaration that the signatories considered it 'highly improper' to give or to accept an invitation to entertainments or assemblies on Sunday, to travel, to exercise worldly occupations or employ domestics or dependents to the detriment of their religious duties. They undertook to refrain from all these activities in future. Some fashionable hostesses were induced to sign; others were indignant; and the Speaker of the House of Commons, who was in the habit of giving Sunday parties, expressed himself forcibly.

Nor were other points of morality neglected, though, judging by their own expressions, one might be pardoned for supposing that Wilberforce and his friends thought them of less importance. In 1800, Lord Auckland and the Bishop of Rochester, a founder-member of the Proclamation Society, made heroic and finally successful efforts to carry a bill in the House of Lords, making it a penal offence for a divorcée to marry the co-respondent, thus causing considerable embarrassment to Lord Holland, the Whig leader, whose own marriage was of this kind. Bishop Porteus supported the bill strongly; his view was that a divorced woman should go into retirement and lead a life of penitence for the rest of her days. In the debate, the law-lord, Kenyon, also a member of the Proclamation Society, was attacked by Lord Carlisle as a 'legal recluse', unfit to decide such a question, and a feud developed. Lord Kenyon quoted the expression in court, saying that he knew as much of human life as he wished and thanked God he had not the knowledge of 'titled adulterers at Newmarket, in Bond Street, and in the stews'.

It was the first serious formal clash between the reformers and High Society, for the question of divorce was a purely aristocratic one at that time, a special act of Parliament being necessary on every occasion. Such acts, none the less, had become frequent and were still increasing. In the end, though Lord Auckland carried his bill in the Lords, it was thrown out in the Commons, where there were no bishops nor even clergy, but plenty of noblemen's nominees.

These years, in fact, brought several defeats to the reformers. They cannot be called set-backs, since it was a remarkable advance that the attempts could even be made. Pitt was unintentionally responsible for another crisis in 1798. Not Wilberforce and his friends alone were horrified when he fought a duel on Putney Heath with an M.P. who considered himself insulted in a debate; the Prime Minister's life was far too precious at that time to be needlessly endangered. But the moral crusaders were more appalled than most, for this was one of the customs they were most determined to abolish—and moreover, 'to complete the horror', as Hannah More says, 'they chose a Sunday!' (The humour is certainly unconscious.)

Wilberforce's immediate reaction was to give notice

of a motion in the House to prohibit duelling. But for once he allowed himself to be overborne. Pitt, who, in spite of his tolerant temperament, would never endure interference in his personal affairs, gave him to understand that he would resign if the motion were carried, and, when Wilberforce found that, on this understanding, only five or six members in the House of Commons would support him, he withdrew it.

Duelling was particularly obnoxious to the religious reformers, not so much because of its essential lawlessness and danger to life and limb, as because it was the ultimate expression of the code of honour by which the upper classes then lived. One of Hannah More's reasons for condemning even tragedies on the stage was they contained 'a prominent thread of false principle', i.e. the standard of honour, as against Christianity. 'Honour is the religion of tragedy.' Wilberforce carried the matter so far in later years as to write a stern letter to his schoolboy son because he had not reported the misbehaviour of a comrade to their tutor. 'The very same principle', he wrote, 'would prompt you when a man, to obey the laws of honour in fighting duels. This is one of the numerous class of cases in which worldly honour teaches one lesson and Christianity another.' Some of the entries in Wilberforce's diary show rather pathetically that he was haunted most of his life by the fear of being challenged and so forced either to disobey his conscience or lose all social credit. The device of the ingenious Horne Tooke, who, by proclaiming loudly that he would never fight a duel, made it impossible for anyone to insult or challenge him without incurring the charge of cowardice, does not seem to have occurred to him. Or perhaps he would not have thought it right to play upon such vain passions.

Because the code of honour was itself something in

the nature of a religion, the victory of the reformers over it was long delayed and never complete. An actual increase in duelling was deplored by the *Anti-Jacobin* in 1805, and Byron, some twenty years later than Pitt's duel, said that he had been mediator or second in at least twenty quarrels, though in each case he claimed to have effected a reconciliation. A clergyman, he said, was the most difficult subject he ever had to deal with, but then 'he was in love'. As late as 1829 the Duke of Wellington, when Prime Minister, repeated Pitt's exploit. Duelling was finally prohibited in the army in 1844 after the political triumph of the Middle Classes in the Reform Act; and this led to its general discontinuance; but the code of honour did not altogether die with it. There was still horse-whipping and fist fighting. And certainly the stigma on 'sneaking' at school has survived to this day. Even when Dr. Arnold had done with him, the English gentleman retained other standards than those of Christianity.

The reformers seem to have been less obtrusive during the first few years of the nineteenth century. But there were signs that the leaven was working. The Speaker's receptions were quietly transferred from Sunday to Saturday evenings in 1801. These were the years of a proliferation of religious societies, with Wilberforce always at the centre—the Church Missionary Society, the Bible Society, The Prayer Book and Homily Society. Sunday schools spread throughout the country, with the aim of having one in every parish. The conspirators now had their own press organ, the *Christian Observer*, founded in 1801. There is a letter from Wilberforce to Hannah More about it in 1802, mildly deprecating his colleague Henry Thornton's invitation to her to contribute an account of a particularly poignant triumphant death-bed, and

47

suggesting rather some religious and moral tales to 'enliven' the magazine a little. 'The truth is, it is heavy, and it will be heavy from the very nature of the case. If it be not enlivened, it will sink.'

He was over-anxious. Though it certainly remained heavy, the *Christian Observer* was still in being in 1816, when the schoolboy, Macaulay, manœuvring his austere father, its editor, with precocious skill, did indeed succeed in enlivening it for a short space, though not without causing some scandal to its subscribers.

Apart from these public manifestations, the reformers carried on vigorous personal missionary work. As an independent M.P., Wilberforce had a wide range of personal contacts. 'Mr. Wilberforce', wrote Hannah More once, 'lives in such profound retirement . . . that he does not see above three and thirty at breakfast!' She described his ante-room as 'like Noah's Ark, full of beasts clean and unclean'. He had also numerous correspondents and was in the habit of giving them commissions to take the spiritual temperature in their respective spheres. An interview with a sympathetic lawyer in 1802 was very satisfactory. Many of the young rising men, he told Wilberforce, had become religious. Sunday consultations were becoming rarer and more lawyers attended public worship. On the other hand, a grieved note to a naval captain remarks that during their meeting he took the name of God in vain, a practice which Wilberforce fears is prevalent in the army and navy. He offers to send him a parcel of bibles and tracts for distribution to the sailors; but there is nothing to show whether the offer was accepted.

Several letters of this kind suggest that the old code of manners still hampered Wilberforce to some extent; he was evidently not always able to voice rebukes at the moment of the offence, but, driven by conscience, wrote letters afterwards. The letters were always as courteous and tactful as the occasion would admit; but even the most delicate situations were not shirked. A wife was severely taken to task for a scolding and domineering attitude towards her husband; in another letter, Wilberforce rebukes his own mother for fretfulness in her old age. The biographers quote these letters, but unfortunately either had not access to the answers or did not consider it part of their task to supply them, so that one is left wondering how effective such protests were. Even Wilberforce's prestige can hardly have made them all acceptable. He must have found it comparatively easy to tackle Boswell, whom he met by chance at a country house, for Boswell would listen to anything; but if he had known his quarry as well as the twentieth-century reader knows him, perhaps even Wilberforce would not have spent his precious time and eloquence on this chameleon. Boswell, indeed, made no difficulty about the doctrine of human depravity; but—very prudently—could not be brought to assent to eternal punishment.

Many converts, in the new encouraging atmosphere, were evidently going about engaged in similar promiscuous proselytising. One young Yorkshireman told Wilberforce that he always 'began warily' by inquiring whether his victim had experienced the new birth. Wilberforce admits that he would hardly get so far in a dozen visits.

If the short peace of 1802-3, when, with a sigh of relief, English society swarmed over to Paris, checked the efforts of the reformers a little, their opportunity soon returned as the pleasure-seekers were chased back—those of them who were not trapped when Napoleon shocked Europe by introducing the uncivilised practice of detaining enemy aliens as soon as war broke out.

The new acute threat of invasion that followed in the next few years was accompanied by an equally acute phase of the conflict between the new Puritans and the worldly—a striking tribute to the vitality of our ancestors who could not even be frightened into mutual harmony. Some people were obviously frightened enough, however, for Lord Radstock recruited 153 members for the Society for the Suppression of Vice (the new name of the Proclamation Society) in 1804. On the other hand, Wilberforce failed this time to prevent the training of the militia on Sundays; Napoleon's army waiting for its transport at Boulogne spoke for the moment more eloquently. He was more successful in 1805, when with his little band of Independents and the help of the Speaker's casting-vote, he brought down Lord Melville on a doubtful charge of corruption ten years old. It was merely good luck that Melville had already so far reorganised the navy, neglected during the Peace, as to make Trafalgar possible the same year, and that he could recommend to Pitt a competent, though aged, successor, Sir John Middleton. Hannah More was delighted at Sir John's succession, but for other reasons. What a comfort it was, she said, to have a Cabinet Minister 'who *prays* for the success of his measures'.

Meanwhile, Bishop Porteus, still a warrior at seventy-five, found a new line of attack on the Sabbath-breakers. It must have given the conspirators great pleasure that an attack on the theatre was economically combined with it. At the King's Theatre it had been customary to carry on Saturday night performances into Sunday morning. But one Saturday night in May, the curtain dropped abruptly at midnight in the middle of the ballet. The bishop had threatened to prosecute the manager if he carried on into the sacred day. The cheated audience did not take this innovation meekly; they swarmed on to the stage, calling for the bishop; the manager was assaulted and rescued with difficulty. Chandeliers, benches, musical instruments were wrecked and a fly crashed, injuring several people. The riot went on to two o'clock. But Porteus had the law on his side and prevailed.

The bishop was also canvassing society ladies about that 'glaring violation of public decency', Sunday concerts, and received an assurance that they would drop the custom in the next season. Clubs were more difficult. There is an anguished letter from the Bishop to Hannah More asking for her prayers just before he was to go to the Prince of Wales to protest against the Sunday meetings of a new club. In this case, he seems to have overestimated the difficulty, for the Prince merely replied affably that he did not see why the club should not meet on Saturdays instead. The old bishop was ill when he made this sally, and it was his last effort. His friends naturally regarded him as something of a martyr.

The 'Society for the Suppression of Vice' was by this time attaining notoriety. Not only the frivolous, but all broadminded people were becoming alarmed by its activities. Sydney Smith, one of the clergymen who still loved the good things of life, but was none the less formidable for his intellect and wit, contributed an article to the *Edinburgh Review* on the subject in 1809. He called the Society nothing less than a combination of informers employing agents who were paid weekly, and were of the type that would naturally accept such an employment. He said that it now consisted of a thousand subscribers, naming some noblemen and bishops among them, and that it had branches in York, Reading and many other large towns. It was developing into a power that might come to supersede law-courts, clergy and police. It used 'violent methods of making men good', compelling them to go to Church, and effecting instant arrest for swearing; so that people were tempted to conform outwardly with inward revulsion. It was likely to become a clearing house for scandal, impertinence and malice; everyone with a grievance, real or fancied, would try to use it as an instrument of revenge. He demanded a declaration that the Society would not receive anonymous accusations.

The added accusation that the Society was attacking the poor man's amusements, and leaving the vices of the fashionable world alone, hardly seems fair, in view of the activities already noted. A final sop admits that some of the members were well-intentioned, but others were unconscious power-seekers.

The article, a typical product of the fanatically liberal mind, so apt to spoil its case by going too far and not sufficiently checking its facts, seems to have had little more effect than the broom of Sidney Smith's own Mrs. Partington, when she tried to sweep back the Atlantic. The Society continued to flourish for some time to come, though it never actually realised his worst fears.

By this time, the first decade of the nineteenth century, some twenty years after the original Proclamation against Vice and Immorality, the open conspirators had made considerable inroads on the nonchalant habits of the eighteenth century; and Voltaire could hardly then have repeated his remark about the absence of the truly devout in England; nor yet, perhaps, about the absence of hypocrites. The upper classes, particularly the women, were not only directly influenced by the examples and writings of Wilberforce and Hannah More and by stiffening public opinion; but they realised that religion in the lower classes was a valuable insurance against revolution. Some of them distributed Hannah More's anti-revolutionary tracts at their own expense. They realised also that, if they were to advocate religion for others with any effect, they must set some sort of example themselves. They went to Church at least once on Sundays; they started schools on their estates; they showed greater respect for the clergy. Above all, they saw to it that their children were brought up in a comparatively austere and religious fashion. The children, unless they belonged to thorough-going reformers like Wilberforce, must have had a puzzling childhood between the teaching of their tutors and governesses and what they could not but observe of the private lives of their parents. One such famous family, owing to its fortunate habit of writing and preserving its lively correspondence, can be seen in midstream, with its friends and dependents, and will be the main subject of the next chapter.

* III *

A SCHIZOID SOCIETY

Me this unchartered freedom tires,
I feel the weight of chance desires.
WORDSWORTH

WHEN Charles Fox as a child wanted to smash a watch, his noble father sighed and said, 'Well, if you must, I suppose you must.'

There is no reason to suppose that most children, even upper-class children, in the eighteenth century were brought up so much in accordance with the progressive principles of the twentieth. Lord Holland's attitude was more typical of the adult society of his class and day. The prevailing spirit of English upper-class society at that time was that of a true aristocracy, 'Do what you will and take the consequences.'

There were few rules, except the flexible ones of good taste. In general, a man must fight a duel, when challenged, and himself challenge when insulted. Everyone must meet his or her gambling debts, if no other. It was proper to be discreet in liaisons; they might be well known to everyone in society, but they must not be flaunted. It was in breaking this rule that the Duke of Grafton laid himself open to the attacks of Junius. Mrs. Sheridan's comments on her husband's amours showed much more indignation that he had clumsily allowed himself to be surprised in a ludicrous scene than that they had occurred at all. On the wife's side, it was incumbent on her to provide her husband with an heir of his own blood before following her own inclinations. If, as in the case of the Melbournes, the heir died and another man's son was left as legal successor, that was unfortunate, but everyone must make the best of it without fuss; and Lord Melbourne was regarded as a boor for not allowing as large an income to his new heir. Sometimes, such situations worked out more satisfactorily. Lady Yarmouth received large legacies from two gentlemen, each of whom believed himself to be her father.

These general rules of civilised behaviour had been imported from the salons of Paris, whence had come the pervading fashionable influence for more than a century—such a line of conduct as is set out in Lord Chesterfield's *Letters to his Son*. But they were never so clearly formulated, nor so generally accepted in England as in France. The famous letters, published after Chesterfield's death in 1773, received a good deal of hostile criticism. Nor was his adoption of the French custom that husband and wife should have separate establishments imitated in this country even in the highest ranks of society. However, a married couple might rarely see one another in the London Season, and it was considered provincial, if not positively vulgar, to invite them out together. The line between what was and what was not permissible naturally wavered a little. When Lady Melbourne allowed her son's mistress to visit him on his death-bed, opinion was against her. It seems odd that such courageous humanity should have been blamed, while so much frivolous laxity was condoned; but no doubt the objection was to the inevitable conspicuousness of the proceeding—the servants and hangers-on could not miss it. For the same reason when a lady in high society expected an illegitimate child, she often went abroad and the birth took place in some secret retreat in France or Italy.

In general, English Society could never be so unaware of criticism, nor so indifferent to it, as French,

since there existed in England a broad social ladder
by which the aristocracy was constantly recruited from
the climbing middle-class, coming from a layer of
society where standards were more traditional and
where genuinely religious families and individuals still
existed. On the other hand, the influence between the
classes was mutual; moral licence and tolerance also
spread downwards.

But if eighteenth-century standards were lax mor-
ally, they were exacting in matters of tone and style.
It was the fashion, even among those who were not
recognised blue-stockings, to be well educated, to read
widely, to appreciate the arts and literature, to know
something of scientific developments, to have an open
mind on every subject under the sun, and to discuss
them all freely. Above all, it was desirable to possess
that graceful insouciance which is the bloom on the
cheek of a high civilisation; and the heroes of society
were those who best realised this ideal.

Lady Spencer's two daughters, the Duchess of
Devonshire and Lady Bessborough, were at the centre
of the most sparkling circle in the London of the
eighties and nineties. They had not been born in the
purple. Their father had been the richest commoner
in England, and their austere mother had brought
them up to do household tasks, to look after the vil-
lagers, to rise and go to bed early, to read the Bible
morning and evening. But they both married very
young into the older aristocracy, and the training of
their childhood quickly melted in the sun of High
Society. Politically, their husbands belonged to the
Whigs, who had been turned out by Pitt in 1784, so
that they had not even the restraint of official position.
As so often in Britain, however, the brilliance was on
the side of the Opposition. Fox and Sheridan fre-
quented the houses of the two sisters and brought there

the young Prince of Wales, just of age in the early eighties, and eager to show in every possible way his independence of and antagonism to his strict and conventional father. Fox and Sheridan were the greatest gamblers of the day, as well as fastidious experts in every other form of dissipation. They were also the most charming and amusing of companions. Fox, indeed, was so charming that even Wilberforce loved him for 'his frank and friendly temper', though one of his correspondents was less susceptible. 'Veracity in him,' he remarked, 'would be inconsistent with the existence of any other possible virtue.'

In spite of all this, Lady Spencer's influence never entirely failed with her daughters. They were too sweet-tempered and too malleable to become open rebels. Besides, she was often useful. She broke the news to the Duke of the Duchess's first batch of unmanageable gambling debts. Later, she was not told of them, nor was the Duchess's husband, until they could be concealed no longer; Lady Bessborough's debts, almost equally disastrous, were likewise kept secret. But even when she was habitually deceived, Lady Spencer was consulted over every formal family move; she often entertained her grandchildren and gave them some wholesome discipline. Her principles still appear, stuck on rather like postage-stamps, in the correspondence of Lady Bessborough. Surviving her elder daughter and the prime of the younger one, she was able to do some salvage work on the next generation.

It was on Lady Spencer's initiative that Selina Trimmer was installed as governess in Devonshire House in 1789. Mrs. Trimmer was very reluctant to let her go. She probably thought the position, even in a ducal family, somewhat derogatory and she would inevitably know something of the reputation of the household which her daughter was to join. It was only a few years since the Duchess's notorious indiscretions when canvassing for Fox at the Westminster election, when she was said to have kissed a butcher. But the family at Devonshire House was not then what it later became. Lady Elizabeth Foster, with whom the Duke and Duchess presently formed a *ménage à trois*, had only just returned from abroad. The only children at Devonshire House were the two young daughters of the Duke and Duchess, Georgiana, aged six, and Harriet, four. Mrs. Trimmer yielded to her good friend, Lady Spencer, who was so strong a supporter of the Sunday School movement; also, no doubt, to the reflection that Selina would be in a position to do good where it was most needed; and the missionary was dispatched.*

But if Mrs. Trimmer had known how the Devonshire household was to develop it seems doubtful whether she would have consented. As time passed, Lady Elizabeth lapsed into a permanent inmate; and, in the next few years after Selina's arrival, there were added to the family, besides a Devonshire heir, two children of the Duke and Lady Elizabeth—Caroline St. Jules and Augustus Clifford; † Corisande de Grammont, a French child refugee; and two older legitimate sons of Lady Elizabeth. Caroline Ponsonby, Lady Bessborough's nervous and impulsive little daughter, was also often with them. On the other hand, the Duchess's daughter, Eliza, of whom Charles Grey was

* Possibly the fact that Mrs. Trimmer had twelve children may also have had some influence.

† The reason for these additions was humane, if not respectable. The children, though unrecognised, were loved and so could not be left abroad when the French Revolution broke out. One may conjecture that the awkwardness of this situation, which must have faced many families, reinforced the moral reformation.

the father, was born abroad and remained there until her father's relations adopted her.

However, by that time, Selina had become very fond of the Duchess, and there were compensations in living in a household where good manners and tolerance were the rule. Her position was not in the least like that of Victorian governesses as the Brontes experienced it. Fanny Burney remarked that Selina was 'treated in every respect as one of themselves'. The Duchess gave her pretty clothes, rather to Lady Spencer's disapproval; and herself apologised when they had differences of opinion about the management of the children; and the Duke sent her special messages in his letters.

Lady Elizabeth Foster, however, Selina never tolerated. Throughout their long, inescapable association they seem to have bristled at each other like angry cats. Even Lady Spencer, who herself loathed Lady Elizabeth and met her only occasionally to keep up appearances, once rebuked Selina for not rising when she came into the nursery.

Whether Selina passed on her prejudice to the two original little girls of Devonshire House, Georgiana and Harriet, or whether from instinctive childish jealousy, they too hated Lady Elizabeth from the first. Lady Elizabeth's own personality certainly did not help. Though she was a success in adult society, even her partisans admitted that she had that defect to which children are always merciless—affectation of manner. This common detestation made a bond between the governess and her first and most important charges and strengthened her influence with them. Apart from this, her life with her pupils cannot have been very easy; but then the daughter of Mrs. Trimmer would neither expect nor want an easy task. She was, according to Fanny Burney, a 'pleasing, but not pretty young woman and seemed born with her excellent Mother's amiableness and serenity of mind'. In spite of appreciating the caps and gowns the Duchess gave her, Selina never succumbed to the atmosphere of her environment. The children called her '*vent de bise*' and '*raison sévère*'.* They joked about her prudishness and enjoyed shocking her. She had a difficult part to play as something like a secret agent for Lady Spencer in the household and there were occasional *contretemps*. A tentative plan to bring in her brother as companion for the young heir faded out under the Duke's opposition. He did not want his household to be so much in the hands of one family, however worthy.

But with Georgiana and Harriet, Selina never lost her influence. Georgiana came to her for backing when, in a phase of girlish piety, she took an aversion to the opera, and wanted to become a recluse, so that the Duchess had to bring forward the argument that, for a duke's daughter, it was a duty to live a public and social life and so help the poor by giving employment —the comfortable old fallacy that is even yet not quite dead. Harriet would write and apologise to Selina when she had to travel on a Sunday, promising to read serious books on the way, and assured her that the thought of her saved her from follies at the most dazzling parties.

As her pupils reached adolescence, Selina's task naturally became more difficult. The boys of the Lamb family, hovering round the girls, made sarcastic couplets about their dragon. Selina disapproved of their family; it was their mother, Lady Melbourne, who had originally initiated the Duchess into the ways of high society, and her own household was almost as

* French was a fluent second language among the English aristocracy of the time.

curiously mixed as the Duchess's own. Nor had the boys come under anything corresponding to Selina's influence. She must have felt it as a failure when one of them eventually married Caroline Ponsonby and another the other Caroline, Lady Elizabeth's daughter. None the less, over the years, Selina became the trusted stay and support of the household she had adopted. As it staggered from one crisis to another, it could never, with her staunch figure present, entirely lose its respectability.

Around young Harriet, a typical specimen of these domestic crises developed after the Duchess's death in 1806. Her beloved elder sister, Georgiana, had been happily married to a well-conducted young nobleman some years before. Selina, rejecting an invitation to become under-governess to little Princess Charlotte, the heiress to the throne, had by this time passed on to be Lady Spencer's companion. The Duchess's death therefore left Harriet at the age of twenty-one at Devonshire House with her father and his mistress, Lady Elizabeth, and no other companion but her younger half-sister Caroline, Lady Elizabeth's daughter, who did not yet know of her own parentage.

It is interesting to find that aristocratic social technique proved quite unequal to this situation. The Duke's own attitude remains conjectural. In the published correspondence of the family, the worried and anxious letters that passed to and fro include no contribution from him. He apparently went his own way quite indifferent to the scandal and embarrassment he was causing. Certainly, he had no intention of parting with Lady Elizabeth. His mother-in-law, Lady Spencer, would not now set foot in the house; and expressed approval when they were excluded from a royal function. As she strong-mindedly observed, such rebukes set a valuable example and they must not expect any

special treatment in their own case.* But she did not
desert her young granddaughter. Though she would
not take her away from Devonshire House, she often
kept her with her whole days, coming specially to
London for the purpose. At home, her good angels
supported Harriet in relays. When there was no one
else Selina would come and stay with her. Georgiana
poured out floods of sympathy and advice by letter
and invited her for frequent visits. Over every development, almost every incident, there were family consultations, decisions, admonitions as to how she was
to behave.

Harriet, who evidently had the happy disposition
of her mother, combined with a sturdier character,
took her predicament with a sweet and rueful seriousness. She tried at first to win over her father, to make
herself important to him—a hopeless effort, since he
had never been much interested in his children and
was not likely to become so now. Lady Elizabeth was
constantly trying to bolster up her position by appear-
ing in public with legitimate members of the family.
Harriet would escape going to the opera with her by
pretending a cold or an engagement to go to Lady
Spencer. Her nightmare was a visit to Brighton, which
Lady Elizabeth threatened to engineer: if they went,
Harriet might not be able to avoid visits to the
Pavilion, or even an introduction to Mrs. Fitzherbert,
the Prince of Wales's mistress.

If Harriet's letters assume, at this time, a slightly
priggish tone, one can hardly blame her. Her aunt,
Lady Bessborough, was also trying to help. She was
often at Devonshire House to keep Harriet in counten-

* Wilberforce attached so much importance to this policy of
the Court in cutting unconventional households that he strongly
recommended it to the negro King Christophe of Hayti. Unfortunately, the King's reply, if any, is not given.

ance. But her own liaison with Granville Leveson-Gower, which was well known, made her support somewhat equivocal. Harriet, writing in confidence to Selina, stigmatised her as an awful example of the results of self-indulgence and shaky principles. At this juncture, she much preferred Selina herself, who became 'my dearest, my best of friends'. She became almost excessively prudish about her own conduct; Lady Bessborough complained pathetically to her correspondents what hard work it was to chaperone a girl who persisted in clinging to her company all the time and how it interfered with interesting conversations.

As the Duke's intention to marry Lady Elizabeth (now a widow) became unmistakable, some way of extricating Harriet had to be found. The obvious one was marriage. She was in her early twenties, already quite a late age to remain unmarried in her time and class; but several tentative love-affairs had come to nothing. After all, it was Lady Bessborough who solved the problem. In typical eighteenth century fashion, she had realised for some years that her own affair with Granville Leveson-Gower was reaching its natural term and had been looking for a suitable match for him. She saw no reason now why her niece should not fulfil this function. There is little about Leveson-Gower's courtship of Harriet in the published letters of the family. His relationship with Lady Bessborough had not excluded other affairs of the heart; in fact, he seems to have been almost as irresistible as Byron, though better balanced. Harriet obviously fell in love with him, and she must have been satisfied that his connection with Lady Bessborough was over. Society speculated on 'the secret articles of the treaty'. In this way, by marrying the man who had already had two children by her aunt, young Harriet escaped from the impossible position in which her parents' indulgences had placed her.

Actually, the marriage was a great success. Leveson-Gower, unlike Byron, was ready to settle down when he married; his charm was of a gentle and amiable quality, and, again unlike Byron, he had a definite career to absorb his energies. He had carried out an important diplomatic mission to Moscow for Pitt and, after the end of the war, was ambassador at Brussels and then, for many years, in Paris. Harriet gradually developed into a great Victorian lady of poise, charm, and dignity, and, what was less usual among Victorian ladies, a surviving sense of humour. She never forgot Selina's teaching; moral and religious reflections of unimpeachable orthodoxy often, though not too often, reappear in her correspondence. She did not, however, entirely cease to find Selina funny. Driving with her in the Park, during the crisis of George IV's scandalous matrimonial affairs in 1821, she reported that Miss Trimmer did not know where to shelter her modesty and that her comments were mostly groans. In her later years, after her husband's death, Harriet took to philanthropic work.

This particularly poignant situation of young Harriet Cavendish near the turn of the century, when she appealed to her brother to marry someone with whom he would want to stay, must have been merely an extreme example of those of many young persons in high society. Many a child's teeth must have been set on edge by the sour grapes that its parents had eaten. Lady Spencer remarked on the exclusion of other doubtful *ménages* besides that of Devonshire House from royal receptions. Constant allusions in the family correspondence show frequent divorces and complicated relations in the comparatively small circle of London society. The resolution of the House of Lords to check the increasing number of divorces seems to have had very little effect, and, if it did anything at all, probably merely increased scandalous situations within marriage.

Another of the children of Selina Trimmer's flock was never placed by circumstances in any position of the difficulty and embarrassment of Harriet Cavendish's; her difficulties were of her own making; and yet she had a far more unhappy fate. The story of Caroline Ponsonby, usually called by her married name of Caroline Lamb, is sufficiently well-known. Of an abnormal sensitiveness, she displayed the dilemma of her generation in its extreme form. Her husband, William Lamb, the future Lord Melbourne, was the eighteenth century type of aristocrat, and eventually lived on to charm young Victoria with his old-world graces. It is amusing to find that, in his youth, he and his brothers were regarded as somewhat too boisterous for refined Society. The tolerance he showed of his wife's vagaries indicate that he would have been perfectly willing to live an upper-class life of the eighteenth century type, with husband and wife pleasantly and agreeably each going his and her own way, when their first enthusiasm for each other —for it was obviously a genuine love-match—had cooled.

Caroline, however, kept no rules, not even those of good taste. She was eccentric and impulsive, but, above all, frank. She never understood polite concealment. Her love-affair with Byron, although conducted with the utmost indiscretion, could have been tolerated—in fact, was tolerated; even her open pursuit of him after he wished to end it might have been lived down. What was impossible to forgive was the publication of her novel, *Glenarvon*, a turgid and lurid account of the whole business with recognisable, though wildly exaggerated, portraits of everyone concerned. Though her husband and her family never entirely abandoned her, she was never again accepted in Society after that. When she asked eighty guests to dinner, only ten arrived. Caroline's career ended in a miserable, neurotic middle-age, kept in seclusion as much as possible by her relations, with sudden spectacular dashes from time to time after some new fancy. She was an embarrassment to the Duke of Wellington, she tried vainly to find compensation in literary and scholastic society, and finally died, exhausted, at forty-six.

It was a curious career for the grandchild of Lady Spencer and the pupil of Selina Trimmer, more especially as Caroline had been a favourite of her grandmother's and very often with her in childhood. But she was also devoted to her delightful, but irresponsible mother, Lady Bessborough, and must have found the contrast confusing. The family were concerned about her instability from a very early age. Lady Spencer remarked about her, during one of her visits when she was sixteen, that she was affectionate, 'without any hurry or fidget', evidently with the idea of reassuring her mother. The younger members of the family regarded her with some contempt, especially as they grew older. And yet Caroline's own writings show that she had acquired the principles of her mentors just as thoroughly as Georgiana and Harriet: she did not commit her sins and follies without realising their nature, but under uncontrollable impulse, and her repentances were of equal violence. On her first meeting with Byron, she had recognised him instantly as 'mad, bad and dangerous to know'; and her love-affair with him followed with fatal promptitude. It was the fascination of perversity and, in Byron, it met its complement.

Glenarvon expresses the conflict and may well have saved its author's reason for the time being. If she really became mad later, as her friends considered, she was not mad at the time she wrote the book. Feverish as it is, it is too coherent to be the work of a lunatic. A passage in the book diagnoses Byron's attitude. Lady Margaret (a caricature of Lady Melbourne) admonishes the heroine about Glenarvon's pursuit of her:

> You are loved more because your ruin will make the misery of a whole family, and your disgrace will cast a shade upon the only man whom Glenarvon ever acknowledged as superior to himself—superior both in mind and person. This, child, is your potent charm—your sole claim to his admiration. Show him some crime of greater magnitude, point out to him an object more worth the trouble and pain of rendering more miserable, and he will immediately abandon you.

This diagnosis probably implies too much deliberation in Byron's perversities—a natural mistake in the circumstances. He was the victim of the same disease as Caroline herself—a split personality. For him, as for her, good and evil had separated sharply off from each other, just as they had for Wilberforce and his friends. There was no light-heartedness about their sinning. Byron's attitude was not the scepticism of the eighteenth century; it was defiance rather than indifference, as the orgies at Newstead Abbey clearly suggest. A genuine agnostic is no more interested in the Black Mass than in the normal one. Byron's wife, in later years, denied that he was an agnostic at all, his 'conscience was always alive'; but his God was a Calvinistic God, the God of vengeance, and hell-fire fascinated him. It fascinated his victims at second hand.

Yet, in many of Byron's letters and even in much of his conduct, where erotic adventure was not involved, he appears as a true son of the Age of Reason. When he was advising his friends, inspecting his young heir, adjudicating on his servants' or tenants' troubles, he was full of good sense and good feeling. He spoke well in the House of Lords against the severe measures taken against starving workmen who had broken up machines; and aroused vain hopes in the Whig leaders. He supported Leigh Hunt and his family of eight for a long time in Italy; and, if he eventually found the situation intolerable, most people would probably have found it so much sooner.* His comments on life and on literature show insight and understanding. Even his constant and involved love-affairs might seem partly palliated by the ingenuous avowal, 'I could love anything on earth that appeared to wish it,' if it had not been written about Caroline Lamb and followed by the cutting addition 'at the same time I do sometimes like to choose for myself'. Susceptibility to boredom, followed by fiendish bad temper, was Byron's curse and that of his victims; when that happened, the fine gentleman vanished and the Satanic double appeared.

In the young cousin of Caroline Lamb's husband, Annabella Milbanke, the new morality tried its hand on the problem so militantly presented by Byron. Annabella's first reaction to him was very different from Caroline's, and very much less perceptive. He was not dangerous to her, she said. He lacked 'that calm benevolence which could only touch my heart' —a surprising understatement. Annabella was the

* According to Leigh Hunt, drinking brought out Byron's best qualities. This, if true, would suggest that his worst ones were also the more superficial, though they did no less execution for that.

only child of a rich provincial family and was pious, learned, priggish and only twenty when she met Byron in 1812. Her aunt, Lady Melbourne, was Byron's confidant and wanted him to settle down in proper eighteenth-century style with a rich heiress, incidentally deterring her daughter-in-law Caroline from her pursuit of him. Like Lady Bessborough, she chose her niece to fulfil this useful function.

Annabella began by rejecting Byron when he proposed. But relations were carried on for over a year by correspondence, because the all-conquering Don Juan was piqued and because Annabella was both fascinated and full of missionary zeal. This correspondence was of a most improving nature, mainly concerned with religion. Each letter on either side was to have been the last; but they went on. Meanwhile, Byron continued from one love to another and finally to the love that never left him, that for his half-sister, Augusta Leigh. As this last was a 'scrape' that disconcerted even Byron himself when it went so far that Augusta had a child by him, he seized the chance of escape as soon as he realised that Annabella's reluctance was not genuine, and his letters make it clear that he sincerely hoped that marriage with her would give him stability. Lady Melbourne, who knew of the incest, evidently gave no word of warning to her brother or to her niece.

Annabella's mission was doomed from the start. Even if the passion between brother and sister had not flared up again, she was far too young and inexperienced for the rôle. Within little more than a year, she was back with her parents and Byron was about to leave England for the remainder of his life.

Thus both the girl who knew he was dangerous at first glance and the girl who thought him not dangerous to her equally had their lives shattered by Byron.

Caroline's was ruined; Annabella picked up the pieces. As long as he lived, she suffered the attacks of her exiled husband, who took ruthless advantage of the fact that she concealed her real case against him, even helping Augusta to pay blackmailers who threatened to reveal it. These attacks were the more effective for being in eloquent verse, published and popular. But there was no moral conflict in Annabella and she therefore survived and made a life for herself, befriending Augusta and Byron's child by her, doing good works, consorting with evangelical clergymen, founding schools and generally assisting the early Victorian social reformers. She even went into Society, in a pathetic attempt to live down the reputation for priggish rigidity with which Byron had saddled her. But there was, as always, a spark of truth in the poet's accusations. Since the brother was out of her reach, Annabella, assisted by a pious friend, attempted the conversion of the amiable, but feckless sister, only to come to the conclusion that Augusta suffered from 'a kind of moral idiocy since birth'. She actually had the idea that any conduct was permissible so long as no one was hurt by it.

But if Annabella was, on the whole, worsted by Byron and his sister and yet again by their daughter, Medora, who sponged on and deceived her, the growing morality of society was not. It drove Byron himself out of the country. It was marking out the sheep from the goats through the first two decades of the nineteenth century. There were now plenty of young converts of the second generation who, like Annabella, knew where they stood, and suffered no serious internal conflict. Hannah More says of Lady Lucy Bury, who visited her, 'She is lovely in mind and in person and, from being a little gay, is become very serious.' She had many such protegées. A clergyman correspondent of hers records the case of a young lady almost persecuted by her aunt for her 'seriousness', who had obtained relief by inducing the aunt to read Hannah's novel, *Coelebs in Search of a Wife*.* She now read what her niece advised.

This incident of the converted aunt occurred in 1810, and, remembering Harriet Cavendish on *her* aunt, one may surmise that it was about this time that children were beginning to reproach their parents for frivolity. Four years later, the *Christian Observer* found it desirable to print an article for the guidance of its young readers on 'The Conduct of Religious Characters to their Parents', for use 'when our beloved parents happen to be insensible to the importance and blessedness of piety'. It had been known to happen, the writer warned, that, through zeal not sufficiently tempered with prudence and charity, young converts had actually increased their parents' antagonism to religion. They must therefore display meekness and tact, and give an example in the constancy of their own conduct, always backed by prayer. They should refer their parents to the Bible itself rather than to other pious works, though indeed one son had prevailed by reading aloud passages from *Practical Christianity* without giving the name of the author, so that when the 'appalling secret' was revealed, they were already half won over. This passage makes one suspect that Wilberforce himself was the author of the article since it seems unlikely that a fellow-worker would have referred to his identity, even jestingly, as an 'appalling secret', whereas a man may easily make such a jest about himself. The conclusion of the article, too, is characteristic of the less attractive side of Wilberforce's faith. If all efforts proved in vain, it runs,

* Even less readable to modern taste than Hannah More's other works.

71

it would be some mitigation of the child's filial grief to
recollect that his parents did not perish through his fault.

It was about this time, too, that Mary Sherwood,
who had had, with interludes, so gay a youth and
loved dancing so much, was finally and completely
converted in India. There, Wilberforce's persistence
had so far worn away the Company's objection to
Christian missions that evangelical clergymen, mainly
Charles Simeon's disciples from Cambridge, were
arriving in numbers. It was their doctrine of 'human
depravity' that brought comfort and conviction to this
eighteenth century parson's daughter. She said that
it explained everything—the nature of the disease and
the remedy. She began to regard cards as 'the devil's
book', would leave the table when a light jest was
made, and danced only under protest when, as a
married woman, she had to start the ball. 'From what
we heard then,' she wrote of 1809, 'we supposed that
since we had left England, the cool green island had
become a land of saints.'

Jane Porter, the novelist, took the same view. 'I
need only call to the mind of Mrs. Hannah More', she
wrote in 1815, 'what was the state of morals and
religious opinions amongst all ranks of person in the
country of twenty years ago. The poor were in profligate ignorance—the rich in presumptuous apostacy.'
When she was a child, she recalls, she once burst into
tears at dinner when some people were scoffing at
religion without a reprimand from anyone. This would
not now be tolerated in any company 'and that was
then considered a respectable circle'.

A letter from Thomas Moore to Leigh Hunt in 1818,
warned him to keep quiet on religion and morality,
'the mania on these subjects being so universal and
congenital that he who thinks of curing it is as mad
as his Patients'.

Yet 1810 to 1820 were the years of the Regency, when it seemed that eighteenth-century freedom and tolerance had worked itself up into a frenzy of perversity and dissipation. Scandals multiplied. Ruined gamblers were everywhere. Duels increased. There was a craze for prize-fighting. Nonchalance attained martyrdom when one buck left a note to say that he had committed suicide because he was tired of buttoning and unbuttoning. The Prince-Regent was described in the *Examiner* of 1812 as 'a corpulent man of fifty . . . a violator of his word, a libertine over head and ears in disgrace, a despiser of domestic ties, the companion of gamblers and demireps'.*

Such a monarch could hardly keep up the restraining influence which his father's court had exercised; he could not refuse to meet divorced persons, even though he kept to his father's custom of excluding them from official functions, to the disgust of his former friends. Perhaps this was what encouraged Wilberforce, as he mentions in a brief note in his diary, to sound the Prince-Regent about this time on the question of making adultery a criminal offence. Unfortunately, there appears to be no further record of this conversation.

Good taste itself was now passing out of fashion. Rude impudence replaced wit. Maria Edgeworth remarked in 1820 that the French complained that, unlike their own young gallants, English dandies would not try to please women even if they could. Freedom to develop personal idiosyncrasy had become a wild licence. One dandy, unable to endure country quiet, had a coach and four driving up and down all night, calling the hours; another was in the habit of putting out candles by throwing pillows at them. Another's

---

* The Hunts spent two years in prison for this; but they were treated as popular heroes.

celebrity depended on his having played ball against the Walls of Jerusalem. The Prince-Regent gave a dinner in which a real stream of water, stocked with goldfish, ran down the table. Beckford outdid Horace Walpole in fantastic architecture; gamblers staked immense sums on the turn of a penny; practical jokes, often cruel ones, were to many the main business of life. Casualties were naturally heavy; some died of drink, some were killed or crippled in duels, many more ruined at the tables. When Dickens and Thackeray in the next generation wanted models for their wicked noblemen, they went back to this period of their childhood. Lord Steyne in *Vanity Fair* was modelled on Lord Yarmouth, one of the Prince-Regent's favourites.

It is no wonder that contemporary observers were bewildered, and alternated between dismay at the licentiousness of the times and complacency at the immense progress of religion and moral reform. While Byron was the lion of the season in 1812, Maria Edgeworth succeeded him in 1813. When Napoleon escaped from Elba, Wilberforce thought the Divine Will had allowed it because the former sufferings he had caused had not brought the intended reformation; and yet, a year or two later, he saw 'in every part of this country new proofs presenting themselves of the diffusion of religion'. Hannah More in like manner thought the death of Princess Charlotte in 1817 a punishment for the national lack of piety and gratitude for deliverance; but the year after she seems to have diagnosed the situation more accurately, 'It appears to me', she wrote, 'that the two classes of character are more decided than they were; the wicked seem more wicked, and the good, better.'

To Hannah More and to an increasing number of her contemporaries life was thus becoming melodramatic, with only two classes of character—the good and the bad. Popular literature had turned the same way. Black and white characters had succeeded the recognisable human beings of Fielding and Richardson and Fanny Burney, with few besides Jane Austen still interested in normal humanity. This was the time of the enormous vogue of Mrs. Radcliffe, a shy and retiring person in private life, who dominated the imaginations of young people for some twenty years with the figures of gallant and virtuous heroes, innocent heroines and black-hearted villains in settings of haunted castles or abbeys among wild mountains and forests. But Virtue was always triumphant in the end. And, as a contemporary admirer put it, in all this lurid business, the author had 'forborne to raise one questionable throb or call forth a momentary blush'.

Mrs. Radcliffe's formula, however, left out the souls still divided in themselves—the Caroline Lambs and the Byrons—and, presently, to the blessed and the damned, was added a third type, an import from Germany, the hero-villain, with his mysterious sins, his blasted beauty and predestined doom, in whom good fought a losing battle against evil. To complement him appeared the erring, but still redeemable heroine. In this type of romance, it was not always quite so easy to avoid questionable throbs, and Lewis's *Monk* had to be expurgated in order to escape banning. None the less, the end was still and always the damnation of the Satanic rebel. Unlike Goethe, the British novelists saw to it that the contract was kept and that the devil got what he had paid for.

This figure of the hero-villain was well established before Byron himself appeared to give it real life embodiment and add *élan* to the vogue. Naturally, *Glenarvon* itself falls into this class; and Caroline Lamb's portrait of Byron attempts to convey the supernatural aura of the man who has sold his soul. She must have been one of the addicts of the romantic novel.

In another sense, also, *Glenarvon* is one of a sequence. In three generations of this famous and vocal family * there were women who wrote novels—the Duchess of Devonshire herself, her niece, Caroline and her grand-daughter, Georgiana Fullerton, whose mother was Harriet Leveson-Gower. None of these novels shows great talent; but they are all the more expressive of their generations for that.

The Duchess's book, *The Sylph*, published anonymously in 1779, is written, like Richardson's novels, in the form of letters and its style is of eighteenth-century formality. It is the story of an innocent girl, brought up in the country, married to a libertine and shrinkingly initiated into the usages of Society, where her virtue is protected by various good mentors until the ruin and opportune death of her husband release her for a worthier suitor. One wonders how this youthful effort—she cannot have been more than twenty-two when she wrote it, though she had been married several years—struck the Duchess later in her career when Lady Spencer's training had receded further into the past. Moral as it is, however, there is little allusion to religion in the book. Its gods are good sense, discretion, modesty and rational behaviour. It contains an attack on Chesterfield's 'rakes upon principle'.

Glenarvon shows the innocent corrupted—good and evil fairly at grips in a single soul. Both in style and subject-matter, it is far wilder and more emotional than *The Sylph* and its moral sentiment is alternating. Calantha, the heroine, wallows in self-condemnation, laced with self-pity, and varied by flashes of fierce

* Legally, of course, they all belonged to different families. But this seems to be a case in which matriarchal descent may reasonably be stressed.

wilfulness. But it is in penitence that Calantha dies, while Glenarvon goes to his lurid death still defiant.

To complete the trio, the keynote of Georgiana Fullerton's *Ellen Middleton*, published in 1844, is struck right at the beginning when the saintly canon of a great cathedral observes a weeping penitent in the congregation and is shortly called to hear her confession. This confession occupies the greater part of the book, which is gloomy, maudlin and pious, ending in a general redemption and the heroine's triumphant death-bed. In this instance, however, the sins are not of a sexual nature, but deceptions of another kind. This novel is the only one of the three in which the author is not obviously the heroine; on the contrary, Lady Georgiana is said by her family chroniclers to have lived a saintly life. Her mother, once young Harriet Cavendish, regretted that the book was quite so mournful.

Virtue conquers in all three novels. But it is in *Glenarvon*, product of the Regency, that an intense and crucial struggle, as experienced by a spirit at war within itself, works through the trite dramatics and the amateurish style. The triumphs of morality in *The Sylph* and of piety in *Ellen Middleton* are sure and easy.

Four years after the publication of *Glenarvon*, the scandals of the period culminated in the divorce proceedings begun by George IV as soon as he became King in 1820. There was no innocent party in this case. Whether Queen Caroline had actually committed adultery or not, she had certainly behaved with such gross indelicacy that the point seemed almost irrelevant. The case in her favour was merely the indisputable misconduct of her husband. Most people took the same view as Jane Austen—'Poor woman, I shall support her as long as I can, because she is a woman and because I hate her husband.' It was, in fact, more than British sense of fairness could stomach to decide against the lesser culprit in favour of the greater. It followed that the hearing of the case—which was in the form of an introduction of a Bill of Pains and Penalties into the House of Lords, and not a court case—involved the washing of royal dirty linen in the greatest possible publicity.

The moralists were horrified. Wilberforce, in accordance with his policy that the Great should 'assume a virtue if you have it not' in order not to set a bad example, tried to stave off the crisis and bring about a private agreement. Like most peacemakers, he merely earned the abuse of both parties and, since the London mob had now enthusiastically adopted the Queen's cause, became, for the only time in his life, definitely unpopular. Particularly painful to him was the point on which the quarrel proved irreconcilable—the omission of the Queen's name, on the King's insistence, from Church of England services. It was not that Queen Caroline felt an urgent need to be prayed for, but that she had fastened on this as a vital point of prestige. With two such principals, negotiations became dangerous to everyone who took part in them, since each was liable to go back on any promise made the day before; and Wilberforce was by no means the only public man who lost credit over them. In the end, everything he had feared took place in a sordid and sensational inquiry into the Queen's private life, and open threats by her counsel to introduce the King's own conduct. It finished when the King's majority fell so low that the bill had to be withdrawn.

It is possible now to see that the moral reformers were making a tactical mistake when they tried to hush the matter up. From their point of view, it did good. They had done their work well enough to ensure that the vast majority of ordinary citizens, as distinct from the mob that had followed the Queen about and made so much noise, were shocked at the whole affair, and, what was more important, thoroughly and finally disgusted with all that was characteristic of a Regency Rake. Even the frivolous themselves wanted to hear no more of it. When the Queen tried to follow up her victory with fresh indiscretions, the lampoonist wrote:

> Our gracious Queen, we thee implore
>   To go away and sin no more;
> Or, if that effort be too great,
>   To go away at any rate.

The staider part of the aristocracy drew away from the compromised set and became more concerned about its own reform. As one of Hannah More's clergyman correspondents put it, the business had stimulated a 'more lively impression of the importance of Christianity among the great'. The more optimistic evangelicals even began to have hopes of George IV himself. Harriet Leveson-Gower, though in a good position to observe, was already behind the times when the year after the royal scandal, she expressed concern for 'eight maiden Lady Somersets', whose mother had become Evangelical and withdrawn herself and them from Society; for a footnote assures us that every one of the eight ladies married well and happily with husbands who shared their mother's views.

Hopes of George IV's conversion were not realised. But that he and, after him, his brother continued to reign for another sixteen years was an anachronism. They reigned because they were in the succession and no responsible person wanted a revolutionary disturbance and because, after all, they had no decisive power. But they were so far from being what the nation wanted that revolution was feared, none the less, several times in George IV's reign, solely on account of his unpopularity. The people had had great hopes of Princess Charlotte, for whom Hannah More had written her *Hints towards Forming the Character of a Young Princess*; but Princess Charlotte died in 1817. William IV was only relatively respectable, but was treated with more forbearance. He was sixty-five when he succeeded, and something better was in sight. At the very time of the scandal of 1820, Wilberforce records a visit to the Duchess of Kent and 'her fine animated child on the floor by her with its playthings, of which I soon became one'. The child was then just two; when, as a young girl of eighteen, she succeeded to the throne, she was long overdue in the mind of the regenerated nation. Victorianism had already prepared the way for Victoria.

THE LEARNED FRIEND

Instruction! child of heaven and earth,
As heat expands the vernal flower,
So wisdom, goodness, freedom, power,
From thee derive their birth.

MARY MITFORD

THE brothers and boy-playmates of the girls whose careers were outlined in the last chapter —that is, of the generation born around 1787, the year when Wilberforce's crusade began, and coming of age in the first decade of the nineteenth century —naturally fell less under the influence of growing piety and stiffening morality than did their feminine counterparts. The tradition of the gay young spark sowing his wild oats died hard, or rather never did die completely. Even in the comparative freedom of the eighteenth century, convention had still lain far more heavily on women than on men and the difference was now becoming accentuated—another recognised symptom of receding civilisation. Also, one may well suppose that counterparts of Selina Trimmer among the tutors of young gentlemen were rare, even though these were often clergymen. As for the public schools, Cowper's savage indictment of them in *Tirocinium* was echoed by all the reformers, who would not send their boys there. As Wilberforce and John Bowdler agreed in private conversation, the schools were inadmissible for their children 'from their probable effects on eternal state'. It was not until 1828 that Thomas Arnold set to work on the public schoolboy.

For the eighteenth century young men of good family, schooldays had been followed by the Grand

Tour of Europe, sometimes after a few terms at Oxford or Cambridge, sometimes at once. In the course of this, he was 'polished' or *décrotté*, the harsher French word so often used by Lord Chesterfield. He acquired French manners and culture and returned ready for the seat in Parliament or other comfortable niche that his family had reserved for him. The war broke down this routine. Young men reaching their late 'teens after the fighting had spread over Europe in the nineties could not make that pleasant progress from Paris down through Switzerland to Italy, with perhaps some visits to the minor courts of Germany, or such other variations as might please them or their guardians. Those of them who were of suitable age at the time seized their chance eagerly in the peace of 1802, only to be chased back or caught by the fresh outbreak of war fourteen months later. Lord Duncannon, Caroline Lamb's brother, got out just in time; Lovell Edgeworth was trapped and did not reach home until Napoleon's defeat in 1814. A number of young gentlemen shared his fate, and some were later used as envoys to the British Government. Meanwhile, they were reported to have set up a centre of dissipation at Verdun, where they were quartered in idleness. It may be supposed that most of them, like Lord Yarmouth, the most conspicuous, helped to reinforce the Regency rakes on their return.

But, already, during the earlier period of the war, a substitute for the Grand Tour had been found. Dugald Stewart, philosopher and mathematician, had acquired a brilliant reputation by his lectures on Moral Philosophy at Edinburgh University, and there, during the last years of the eighteenth century and the first of the nineteenth, went many of the more intelligent youths of the nobility and gentry to sit at his feet. Two future Prime Ministers, Lord Palmerston and Lord John

Russell, were among them and two other prominent statesmen of the future, John Ward and Lord Henry Petty, later Lord Lansdowne. Sydney Smith arrived there indirectly from the same cause, in that the squire's son to whom he had been appointed tutor could not go to Weimar, as had been intended. Native Scottish talent profited and extended its influence through this incursion. Henry Brougham made friends with Lord Henry Petty, who later obtained for him a pocket borough as his first seat in Parliament. Jeffrey and Sidney Smith started the *Edinburgh Review* together in 1802.

The two younger boys of the Lamb family, on the other hand, had the originality to go to Glasgow instead, where Professor Millar, who lectured on Law and called poetry 'a mere jingle that proves no facts', also had considerable prestige. They lived with their tutor and did not appreciate the régime of low living and high thinking. 'One of the Miss Millars is pretty,' wrote Frederick Lamb, 'but they are all philosophers and the eldest is exactly like Miss Trimmer.' Perhaps this was why the Scottish inoculation did not 'take' with them. Perhaps the influence of their mother, Lady Melbourne, would in any case have been too strong. However that may be, the future Lord Melbourne remained in all essentials an eighteenth-century gentleman.

Byron characteristically refused to be cheated of his continental tour, and, skirting the war to the south, went through southern Spain and Italy to Greece and the Levant. The irrepressible Henry Brougham, to whom, as a native, Edinburgh was no adventure, also achieved his travels, though somewhat late. He skirted the war to the north through Scandinavia, where he was shocked at the Frenchified court of Stockholm, and even entered Germany and saw Napoleon, while posing as an American. But most young men who were not soldiers remained meekly in Britain and their education became insular with an increasing Scottish flavour. John Ward, heir to the Viscounty, at the age of twenty-seven in 1808, said that he had never set foot out of the country.

Sir James Mackintosh, the great lawyer, said that Dugald Stewart's lectures at Edinburgh had 'breathed the love of virtue into whole generations of pupils'. While it may be doubted whether any course of lectures, however eloquent, is capable of accomplishing this feat, the professor's immense influence is beyond question. In their printed form, the lectures on Moral Philosophy hardly explain this. But they were not printed verbatim; the introduction states that the object in publishing was to give a clear outline, so that the lecturer need keep less rigidly to the point in the spoken versions. Even so, their matter is surprisingly uninspiring. Stewart's triumph was evidently one of personality. There must have been a glamour about him. Most people represent him as extremely handsome, but Henry Cockburn, in a detailed description, says that he was

> about middle size, weakly limbed and with an appearance of feebleness which gave an air of delicacy to his gait and structure. His forehead was large and bald, his eyebrows bushy, his eyes gray and intelligent, and capable of conveying any emotion from indignation to pity, from serene sense to hearty humour; in which they were fully aided by his lips which, though rather large perhaps, were flexible and expressive. The voice was singularly pleasing.

Scott refers to his 'striking, impressive eloquence which riveted the attention of even the most volatile student'.

Remembering the insignificance of Garrick at rest, one can understand why Stewart's pupils received an impression of grace and beauty. To Henry Cockburn, even though visually unhypnotised, the lectures 'were like the opening of the heavens. I felt I had a soul . . . they changed my whole nature.'

Like that of the great actors, before the invention of the gramophone and the cinematograph, Stewart's radiance is lost to later generations. But the published version of his lectures at least enables one to discover what principles were taught in this impressive manner to the young men who came to Edinburgh to hear him. On the whole, it was the familiar common-sense morality of the English philosophical school. Among the various views of older philosophers—the identification of morality with enlightened self-interest, with the love of beauty and good taste, with social training and so on, Stewart voted for Hutcheson's particular moral sense, inborn and incapable of analysis into anything simpler, showing a man plainly his duty to God, to his neighbours and to himself. In these lectures, there is hardly more than a bow to orthodox theology. The existence of God is assumed, but He is rarely mentioned. Nothing is said that would not be as acceptable to a Moslem, a Jew, or a Deist as to a Christian.

Stewart's belief in the special moral sense dovetailed neatly with Paley's arguments for 'natural religion' as given in his *Evidences of Christianity*, published in 1794. He agreed with Paley's view that a man's sense of duty is independent of God's commands and would not be nullified by disbelief in a future life. The Evangelicals, on the other hand, regarded Paley's book with distrust, and Wilberforce censured it because it undertook to prove the truth of Christianity by rational argument. Mrs. Sherwood confirms his misgivings when she says that it suggested to her in her youth the

first doubts of the Christian religion that ever occurred
to her.

One might suppose that, given the moral sense as a
part of a man's natural equipment, he might leave his
moral decisions on each particular occasion to intui-
tion; but Dugald Stewart was none the less in favour
of a definite plan of conduct as part of one's duty to
oneself, and, incidentally, as the only way to happiness. He himself favoured the Stoic course, which he
understood in the original classic sense, not merely as
fortitude in adversity, but as acquiescence and co-
operation in the natural and normal order of the
world. Thus it did not, for him, rule out reasonable
enjoyment of the good things of life.

There was nothing new in all this, and it is difficult
to see why anyone's outlook should have been trans-
formed by it. Some contemporary critics, in fact,
accused the lectures of vagueness and superficiality.
But, no doubt, the young men, like their sisters, were
bewildered by the unstable moral climate in which
they were growing up and were in search of an anchor,
while Evangelical religion would not come so easily to
them with their wider education and greater experience of life. Dugald Stewart did not make such demands upon them. He seems to have shown some bold-
ness in practically ignoring Christianity, since the
Scottish Church had never relaxed its grip as had the
English. Sydney Smith, who had been reluctantly
ordained under family pressure, remarked with envy
on the prestige of clergymen in Scotland, while in
England, they were no more regarded 'than cheese-
mongers'. In this atmosphere it is hardly surprising
that Stewart was presently suspected of sympathy with
the French revolutionaries, since this was at that time
the fate of anyone who showed any kind of un-
orthodoxy.

But if Dugald Stewart's moral outlook was far from being like that of Wilberforce or Selina Trimmer, it had an important point in common with it. If not completely 'serious' in their sense, it was serious enough in the ordinary meaning of the word. The young men who sat under him came away from Edinburgh with a social conscience hardly less grim than the religious conscience of the Evangelicals. No one of his pupils, said Henry Cockburn, could ever be false to his principles without feeling guilty at the memory of Stewart.

Dugald Stewart was the original magnet, but not the only attraction of Edinburgh in the late eighteenth and early nineteenth centuries. To others besides students, it offered the most interesting alternative to foreign travel during the Napoleonic wars. It had its scenic and architectural beauty, quaint old customs and a picturesque dialect. A succession of great men rose opportunely, stimulating and stimulated by the cultural ferment. Native poets from Burns to Scott appeared. Stewart, himself a sociable man, was supported by a talented wife who knew how to run a salon, and there were others of equal attraction. In short, Edinburgh became a place of pilgrimage to the cultured classes in those years. Lord Webb Seymour, one of Stewart's young men, was so happy there that he stayed for the rest of his life. Nor, though a state of desolate virtue prevailed every Sunday, did the city at other times lack jolly taverns, roistering parties or any other facilities of the gay life. Sydney Smith, marooned later in a derelict Yorkshire parsonage by the Clergy Residence Act, wrote nostalgically of his time in Edinburgh. 'Never shall I forget the happy days passed there . . . amidst odours, smells, barbarous sounds, bad suppers, excellent hearts and most enlightened and cultured understandings.' The bad suppers may perhaps be taken as typical of the shift from French to Scottish culture.

The spiritual diet also differed. As always, the pervading atmosphere was that of metaphysics and law. Scotsmen, Smith remarked, even made love in metaphysical terms. He had overheard a young woman say to her escort, 'What you say, my Lord, is very true of love in the aibstract, but——'

Nearly all the talented young Scotsmen of this time began as lawyers—Jeffrey, Brougham, Scott, Lockhart, 'Christopher North'—and their interests were predominantly legal, political, social and economic. Scott was a member of the famous Speculative Society, but he found only moderate scope there for his romantic enthusiasm. More typical subjects for debate were public support for the poor, established religion, systems of taxation, the Slave Trade, the usefulness or otherwise of belief in a future life, Parliamentary Reform. The modern science of Economics, then called 'Political Economy', had been founded by a Scotsman of the previous generation, Adam Smith, to whom Pitt had said, 'We are all your scholars.' This—'the dismal science'—presently became the main speciality of the Edinburgh School. By the time the city was claiming the title of 'The Athens of the North', the glamour was already passing and some of Edinburgh's own brilliant sons were the first to laugh at the claim. 'If Athene had been the goddess of printing rather than that of wisdom,' said Lockhart, 'the title would have been deserved.' Some fifteen years later than Sidney Smith, he describes Edinburgh society less sympathetically:

> The best table-talk was, and probably still is, in a very great measure made up of brilliant disquisition—such as might be transferred without alteration to a professor's note-book, or the pages of a critical Review—and of sharp word-catchings,

ingenious thrusting and parrying of dialectics, and all the quips and quiblets of bar pleading. It was the talk of a society to which lawyers and lecturers had, for at least a hundred years, given the tone.

Lockhart was inclined to be a hostile critic, being ultra-Conservative, while the great majority of Scottish intellectuals were Radical, but it is clear that, by the time he wrote, the brief glory of Edinburgh as a centre of culture was fading. Apart from the reopening of the continent of Europe after the war, Cockburn ascribed the decline to the dying out of the older generation and the rise of a youth 'with little literature and a comfortless intensity of political zeal'.

The peculiar brand of seriousness which the Edinburgh School contributed to the increasing seriousness of the early nineteenth century was thus one of reforming and progressive principles—social and political rather than personal. A glance at Brougham's youthful correspondence or at Lockhart's *Life of Scott* dispels any idea that the 'love of virtue' which Dugald Stewart breathed into his students necessarily involved sober habits of living. Theirs was, however, a jollity more boisterous than elegant. For Henry Brougham and his friends, dissipation seems to have been in somewhat crude alternation with bouts of intense study and hard work, a very different matter from the insouciance of fashionable eighteenth-century society or its perversion in the Regency rakes.

Besides Dugald Stewart's morality, these young men had a battery of new social theories, contributed by contemporary thinkers. They had Adam Smith's economics or their own variations of them. Cockburn says that the young of his time 'lived upon' Adam Smith. They had Malthus' doctrines on problems of population. They had also Bentham's Utilitarianism and its effective slogan, 'the greatest good of the greatest number', without apparent consciousness of its equivocal nature.*

This they applied particularly to the unlimited Scottish faith in the power of education. With James Mill, one of the oldest of them, they believed that when everyone could read, everyone would listen to reason and that then universal suffrage would bring good government. There was a genuine likeness to the Athenian, or, at least, to the Platonic attitude, in the immense confidence which these men placed in the power of rationality. To them, man was neither the original sinner, nor the emerging ape, and they accordingly left out a good deal in their plans for him. Like Socrates, they supposed that men erred only because they knew no better; teach them better and Utopia would be in sight. Believing this, they developed a drive hardly less powerful than that of the evangelical Christians.

When Plato constructed his *Republic*, he did so at a safe literary distance; he put it in a dialogue, Socrates talking to his disciples, half playfully as usual, framing the ideal state as a free exercise of the mind. Yet even Plato was tempted once to try to apply his prescription. The Scottish school meant business from the first. They intended that their plans should be applied, and in course of time many of them were, sometimes with disconcerting results. Meanwhile, the fashion of creating 'systems', as Peacock called them, grew and spread. The early nineteenth century was buzzing with them and no system-maker could see why his well-argued conclusions should not be applied to his fellow-countrymen immediately. In this field, some of the religious reformers kept steadier heads than Dugald Stewart's rationalist pupils, reminding one of Freud's view that in accepting a communal neurosis one may escape a

* Which 'greatest' is to have priority.

personal one. One of Hannah More's pious correspondents quotes Archer-Shee's *Rhymes on Art:*

> *What shapes of social order rise refined*
> *From Speculation's crucible combined,*
> *While cool state chemists watch the boiling brim,*
> *And life's low dregs upon the surface swim!*
> *What though midst passion's fiery tumults tost,*
> *A generation's in the process lost?*
> *Regardless of his raw material, Man,*
> *The calm philosopher pursues his plan.*

In Henry Brougham the Scottish School let loose a
gadfly on the older generation of the Whig aristocracy.
He was no aristocrat himself, but he belonged to a
rising legal family and had been welcomed into aca-
demic circles in Edinburgh on account of his great-
uncle Robertson, the historian. He was an outstand-
ingly clever man. As a student, he wrote mathematical
papers that were published by the Royal Society; and
in his early twenties he produced a large book on
Colonial Policy, of which he had no first-hand knowledge whatever. 'Clever' is, in fact, the right word for
him, since, for reasons of national psychology, it has
come to suggest limitations as well as capacities. He
possessed that comprehensive type of brain that can
absorb anything and everything to just the degree of
depth that both impresses and flatters the average
mind, since it is able to follow with a sense of enlightenment, yet without too much effort. He had also the
bold personality and actor's equipment, including a
prodigious voice, necessary to make the most of his
wares. He was very successful with juries and still more
so with the public. In middle life he became the
first of the great demagogues of modern times. Wilkes,
some forty years earlier, had caused a great stir, but
there was never any question of his taking the lead or

influencing national policies. Now, such leadership was becoming possible, even though the extension of the franchise was still delayed. The Christian reformers and Wilberforce in his Slave Trade campaigns had done much to forward this development by organising mass petitions and using the Press, which could shake even the unreformed Parliament. They had not, of course, had any clear view of the further consequences of this policy. Brougham seized upon their methods and exploited them with complete deliberation.

By subtler minds and more refined tastes, he was regarded with more reserve, often ending in distrust and dislike. He was, on the whole, well received by London society when he arrived there in 1805. They regarded him as something of an oddity; but oddities were still tolerated by high society for their value as entertainment. When he set fire to the powder-horn while out shooting and burnt off his eyelashes, and then proceeded to explain the scientific principles of the explosion, his companions collapsed in helpless laughter. 'We Edinburgh-bred gentlemen ought not to meddle with field sports,' commented John Ward. It was a greater handicap that, as the same observer remarked, affectation was 'the crying sin of all Scotch-bred men of talent', except Stewart and Playfair. Their manners were criticised by the older French-schooled generation. Lord Egremont had not approved of the Scottish year for William Lamb, who was generally believed to be his son. He thought the atmosphere in the Millars' house was too disputatious. Scotch universities, he said, were very much calculated to make a man 'vain, important and pedantic. . . . This is naturally the case where there is a great deal of reading.' In his view, one should let neither study nor the world get too great a hold upon one.

Brougham was an extreme type in this as in other

respects. In spite of the licence granted to oddities, his flamboyant manners and pedagogic dissertations did not always please the great Whig hostesses. He had not the right touch for the salons. According to Harriet Martineau, describing him at a later age, he had a special manner for silly women, but was at a loss with the other kind. The quarrel with Holland House, however, was hardly his fault; his mother had refused hospitality to Lady Holland, travelling in the North, on the grounds that there was a young unmarried girl in the house. A feud with Lady Holland was a considerable handicap to an ambitious young Whig politician.

On the other side, men of solid attainments found Brougham wanting. Though he mastered the science of Political Economy in short order to his own satisfaction in 1816, because the party needed an expert, Hutcheson and Ricardo overwhelmed him in debate on the subject a few years later. He was, however, irrepressible. New schemes, new ideas sprang up immediately after every defeat. Such was his mental restlessness and the eccentricity of some of his notions, that, throughout his life, friends frequently expressed fears for his sanity, as had his own family in his student days. It is an amusing comment on the layman's idea of what constitutes mental disease* that he attained a serene and dignified old age until his death at ninety.

In the early nineteenth century, it presently became almost the most troublesome problem of the Whig Party what to do with Brougham. If it had not been for the friends among the younger Whigs whom he had acquired in student days in Edinburgh, it seems likely that he would never have achieved a political

---

* Melbourne, however, knew better. Talking of Brougham, he told Queen Victoria that a man who was always odd never really went mad.

career at all, and that if he had not been the strongest influence in the *Edinburgh Review*—the first and most powerful of its kind—the career would have come quickly to an end. As it was, he obtained no seat in Parliament until 1810 when he was thirty-two, a late beginning at that time; and he was out again between 1812 and 1815. It is characteristic of him that his return for Winchelsea in 1815 was considered to be an act of revenge on the part of Lord Darlington for a slight from the Prince-Regent.

Once in Parliament, Brougham joined 'The Mountain' * a turbulent left wing of the Whig Party, which had recently developed in semi-rebellion to the old aristocratic leaders. These gentlemen, especially when snatches and possibilities of power returned to them after the long Tory ascendancy under Pitt, were being forced to realise that they were no longer the Progressives of British politics. A louder, more insistent, more business-like—in short, more middle-class—faction was by-passing them. While Parliament remained unreformed, these new progressives could never obtain a majority in the Commons, but they could sometimes command the casting vote, and they could use the new techniques. On the other hand, it was not to their interest to break altogether with the old Whigs, without whom they could never put through any measure. The result was uneasy bargaining and compromise, with Brougham as the *enfant terrible*, liable to create an insufferable awkwardness at any moment. Even his colleagues in 'The Mountain' sometimes found him impossible to work with.

Besides the new methods of petition and press

* Like the modern 'right' and 'left' in politics, the term 'The Mountain' came from the layout of the French Chamber, i.e. extreme revolutionaries were seated at the highest point in the Chamber.

Brougham made use of his legal ability. The Whigs could keep him out of a Parliamentary seat at times, but they could not keep him out of the news, nor even always out of the House, since the chief malcontents who got into trouble with the repressive laws of the time chose him as counsel for the defence. He stated the Liverpool Merchants' case against the Order in Council restricting their trade, he defended the libellers of the Prince-Regent; throughout the long quarrel between the Prince and his wife, he acted as her legal adviser, and was the star performer at the trial of 1820.

Brougham was finally regarded as a failure because he never attained a higher position than that of Lord Chancellor. To this extent, royal and aristocratic opposition, combined with his general capacity for making enemies, frustrated his career. Lord Melbourne, who had proved immune to Scottish education, could not endure him and, after one experience, saw to it that he never held office again.

As a transformer of Society, however, there is no question of Brougham's immense success. The changes were coming, but they certainly came much faster for his efforts and they largely followed his direction. He was often accused of extravagant ambition and devious practices even by his closest colleagues and there seems to be no doubt that the accusations were justified; but, whether from the youthful imbibing of Dugald Stewart's principles or by native grace, he never betrayed the popular cause. All his movements, with whatever détours, made in the direction of progressive reform. The masses recognised this and loved him for it. They knew that he was their friend and no efforts of his enemies succeeded in changing this conviction. Their sheer weight behind him carried him through and over his numerous mistakes.

His greatest work was done, after all, outside Parliament. It was the spread of education on which the Scottish school set its best hopes. 'To diffuse useful information, to further intellectual refinement, sure forerunner of moral improvement,' he proclaimed at Glasgow University, 'to hasten the coming of that bright day when the dawn of general knowledge shall chase away the lazy lingering mists, even from the base of the great social pyramid—this is indeed a high calling in which the most splendid talents and consummate virtues may well press onward eager to bear a part.' There is an ominous presage of modern political and journalistic jargon in the rounded period with its rising sun and onward march; but Brougham was aiming at a new public who were not connoisseurs in style.

The knowledge that Brougham and his associates were intent on diffusing was, however, of another kind than the orthodox classical education of the eighteenth-century upper classes, which was Latin, Greek, Mathematics and nothing else. The lively minds of the Age of Reason had had many new ideas about education, as about everything else, and, though they had not penetrated the public schools or the general practice of tutors and governesses, they had influenced parents of a progressive disposition. But for the mass education of the masses, any subtleties or refinements were ruled out. There was neither time nor money for them. Let the people just be taught to read, thought Brougham and his friends in the early years of the century; then all the rest would follow.

An enthusiast with a system arose to meet the need. Joseph Lancaster, a young man almost without resources, invented the Monitor system, by which one educated schoolmaster could run a school of many hundred pupils simply by a relay method of handing down information. He taught the older children; they passed on the lessons to the younger. Economy was the essence of the plan. Slates and trenches of sand took the place of paper; tabulated facts were posted on the walls; items were memorised by the children chanting in unison. Only reading, writing and arithmetic were attempted in the first place. The older children kept the younger in order. Since Lancaster was a Quaker and could not countenance corporal punishment, offenders were publicly humiliated by being shackled, washed if they were dirty, made to walk backwards. Prizes were given and, in this, no economy was practised; but no one paid fees unless he wished. The principle of delegation was carried so far that soon lads of sixteen and seventeen were organising large schools.

Such whirlwind methods were very congenial to Brougham, who was always in a hurry. He and his colleagues infiltrated into the 'Royal Lancastrian Institution', of which George III had become a patron. Lancaster and his original backers were nonconformists, acting under religious inspiration, but, as they were of various sects, had avoided any sectarian teaching, while making the Bible and pious books the usual reading in the schools. This was good enough for the Scottish radicals, who were concerned with reform in this world, but had no scruples about some small pandering to the religious enthusiasm without which little could be effected by this time. As Utilitarians, they thought religion had its value for social purposes, and, when their oracle, Bentham, aired his agnostic views, he did so under another name. 'There is a vast amount of religion in the country,' wrote Brougham in a letter. 'Some Church Establishment this feeling must have, I am quite clear that a much-reformed Church of

England is the safest form. . . . It is a quiet and somewhat lazy Church.' But he often found, in practice,
that the Nonconformists who, like most minorities,
were in favour of tolerance, were easier to work with.
However, the inference that he himself had no strong
religious convictions is obvious.

The tone of the 'Royal Lancastrian Institution' soon
began to alter accordingly. The prophet Lancaster,
who had actually managed to project a mystic fervour
into his conveyor-belt system of putting information
into children's heads, went the way of most prophets,
having a difficult temperament and no financial sense.
His 'Institution' was taken from him in 1814 and
became 'The British and Foreign Schools Society',
with Brougham as its moving spirit.

But, in the meantime, through the efforts of the
vigilant Mrs. Trimmer, a rival, Dr. Bell, who had
evolved a similar system while teaching in India, but
had no idea of leading a crusade, was dug out of his
comfortable vicarage, and the Church of England
made its reply in the 'National Society for Promoting
the Education of the Poor in the Principles of the
Established Church'.

It was this conflict of the sects that chiefly hampered
Brougham in his fight for the education of the people,
and incidentally contributed to frustrate his career.
The Practical Christians had wanted the people to
learn to read, but only in order to read the Bible, the
prayer-book, and their own tracts. Wilberforce never
lost a friendliness for Brougham because of his zeal for
the abolition of the Slave Trade, but he was alarmed
by schemes for spreading non-religious instruction. He
wavered in his early support for Lancaster. Nor could
he approve of the factory schools founded by Owen,
the free-thinker, in Scotland, which were intended to
render 'manufactures and morals compatible', because

they had no religious basis. Socialistic and rationalistic tracts were now so widespread among the new class of factory-workers that Sunday-school promoters were beginning to wonder, as Mrs. Sherwood confessed, what they had done when they taught the people to read.

In this atmosphere, Brougham's endeavours to pass educational measures in Parliament were baffled again and again in committee or in the House of Lords by the opposition of the bishops. Or sometimes it was the hostility of the Dissenters, afraid that the Established Church might gain some new advantage.

Outside Parliament, he accomplished a great deal. Besides his part in the 'British and Foreign Schools Society', he founded an infant school himself on Owen's model; he harassed the enemy by exposing abuses in Educational Trusts, which were mostly in the hands of the Church; he joined Birkbeck in starting technical institutes for artisans. London University, founded on a non-sectarian basis, was known as 'Brougham's Patent Omnibus'.* To this, Wilberforce's party, now generally known as 'The Saints' or 'The Clapham Sect', retorted with King's College.

But Brougham's particular instrument, his chosen medium of expression, as the 'Proclamation Society' had been Wilberforce's some forty years earlier, was 'The Society for the Diffusion of Useful Knowledge'. It was founded in 1827, about twenty years after Lancaster's method had begun to spread. The logic of it was obvious. Many of the people could now read; they must therefore be given the right things to read. The material must be useful, not the futilities taught in the public schools. As copious as its founder, the Society accordingly began to pour out an avalanche of information in cheap primers, text-books, pamphlets on

* A pun on the University's motto.

every conceivable subject. Already in 1823, Hannah
More had found herself confronted with a small child
who told her that she was reading the 'whole circle
of the Sciences' and it cost half a crown. Another,
asked if she knew her catechism, said that she was
learning syntax. The old pioneer was aghast. Where
would it end? she asked. The common people would
become like the educated Athenian rabble, turbulent and ungovernable, always looking for 'some new
thing'.

The 'Society for the Diffusion of Useful Knowledge'
got to work on a regular series in 1829. The first
'treatise' was by Brougham himself on the 'Objects,
Advantages and Pleasures of Science' and the first
nineteen volumes were all on scientific subjects. Later,
there were also histories and biographies, but the
scientific bias was maintained, and such lighter matters
were usually relegated to an offshoot, 'The Library of
Entertaining Knowledge'. Each treatise was issued at
6*d*. and consisted of thirty-two octavo pages, which, it
was claimed, contained the matter of a hundred ordinary octavo pages. (No one seems to have considered
the matter of eyesight.) If one treatise did not exhaust
the subject, there would be a sequel. A strangely mixed
series resulted. Some of the authors knew how to write,
others did not. Some had the gift of clear exposition;
others would probably baffle a graduate of modern
times. An invitation for offers of 'literary assistance'
suggests that there was some difficulty in keeping up
the supply.

Many people—especially, of course, people who
would have had an education, anyhow—laughed at
the Society for the Diffusion of Useful Knowledge and
its offspring, *The Penny Cyclopædia*. It became Peacock's
'Steam Intellect Society' and Brougham, 'the learned
friend'. But these enterprises could not have succeeded

if there had not been an immense demand for their wares.* As Mackworth Praed wrote:

> *The schoolmaster's abroad you see,*
> *And when the people hear him speak,*
> *They all insist on being free,*
> *And reading Homer in the Greek;*
> *The Bolton weavers seize the pen,*
> *The Sussex farmers scorn the plough,*
> *One must advance with other men;*
> *And so I'm not a Tory now.*

But the leaders of the working-men believed Brougham's gospel, that they would never improve their position without political power, and that they could not handle political power until they were educated. They could not know what education was until they had it, and could only accept what their mentors prescribed. Such a torrent of crude miscellaneous information was the natural result and perhaps the only way in which a beginning could be made.

In spite of such fantastic manifestations, it was due to Brougham and his fellow Utilitarians that something of eighteenth-century humanism survived to leaven the lump of Victorianism—something of reasonableness, tolerance and open-mindedness. They preserved an alternative to the piety of the Saints, with its desire to suppress everything that might conceivably distract human beings from preoccupation with the Four Last Things. They checked the 'Society for the Suppression of Vice' when it brought criminal actions against agnostic and radical writers. Joseph Hume, one of those persistent watch-dogs who have constantly recurred in the House of Commons since the days of

* Even so, *The Penny Cyclopædia* ultimately bankrupted its parent organisation.

Hampden, found his chance to bring the whole character of the Society into question in 1823. The occasion was the case of Mary Carlile, a young woman
who was imprisoned for distributing a tract which—
quite reasonably and moderately—argued against the
divine origin of the Christian religion.

The Society, said Hume, had published no list of
members since 1807, though they had supplied names
to him on his request. There were 250 members, some
of them his own friends, public men of high standing,
peers, M.P.s and all other respectable classes. The
proceedings of these gentlemen advertised the principles they were trying to suppress. In this instance,
the woman's defence had been silenced from the
Bench, as was becoming the custom, and she had been
punished on principles that would not have been acted
on fifty years before. A bill should be introduced to
define blasphemy instead of leaving the question to a
judge and jury. The present method was tyranny and
an infringement of free discussion. Sir Francis Burdett
added to this that the Society could now ruin anyone
merely by a prosecution, even an unsuccessful one.

The debate circled round the possibility or impossibility of defining blasphemy, Wilberforce making the
point that, if there were people who wanted to go as
near the line as possible, he hoped they would overstep
it and be caught. He said that the Society had brought
thirty-two prosecutions and never failed; and con-
cluded by hoping that the woman, Mary Carlile,
would receive divine mercy. Human mercy she could
not have, lest other offenders be encouraged. Hume,
having by a slip of the tongue that would have pleased
a psycho-analyst, called the Society, 'The Society for
the Promotion of Vice', had the wit to make capital
from his mistake.

At that moment the champions of freedom could do

nothing decisive, but they kept such issues alive and never left the Saints a clear passage; and their turn came later when the Whigs came back to power. What ultimately became of the Society for the Suppression of Vice, the author has been unable to discover. Perhaps it faded out when the Evangelicals were called upon to face a different kind of enemy in the eighteen-thirties—the Oxford Movement, and the subsequent stream of conversions to Rome, in which two of Wilberforce's own sons were carried away. But the Society had done its work; the people had been brought to take their religion seriously. A correspondent of Bishop Butler consoled himself in the bitter conflict of the sects, that, whereas in his youth the quarrels had been about the truth of Christianity, now they were about the right form of Christian worship.

The minority of rationalists, who evidently seemed negligible to this clergyman at this juncture, meanwhile remained more interested in this world than in the next and pushed on with their social schemes. But they did not escape the univerally encroaching solemnity. They took themselves as seriously as did the Saints. After Sydney Smith, to whom his fellow-Whigs dared not give a bishopric when they had the power, on account of his wit, the light touch departed from them. The propagandist wit of Brougham and Macaulay took its place. Everything was judged by its purpose and not on its merits. Mary Mitford's ode, *The March of Mind*, quoted at the beginning of this chapter, which was pronounced in 1815 at the first anniversary of the 'British and Foreign Schools Society', was received with a three times three toast, and a flourish from the Duke of Kent's band—to the innocent delight of the author.

This strong rationalist element that persisted in the population throughout the Victorian Age, producing

the kind of man of whom Tennyson made the extraordinary statement:

> *There lives more faith in honest doubt,*
> *Believe me, than in half the creeds.*

shared the Puritanical austerity of Victorian religion,
reversing Wilberforce's dictum that 'a religious man
might sometimes be facetious' in showing that a
rationalist might be as serious-minded as the most
rigid Christian.

THE MODEL CHILD

Leave let me take to place before her sight
A specimen portrayed with faithful hand,
Full early trained to worship seemliness.
WORDSWORTH

IN a mischievous mood, Henry Brougham once told the upper classes of his day, when they were show-ing perturbation about the likely results of edu-cating the 'lower orders', that they could maintain their superiority by working harder themselves.

Whether this motive played any great part or not, children at the end of the eighteenth century began, for good or ill, to undergo a concentrated attention from their elders. Many of these elders had, of course, become more conscientious generally; others felt that, while it was too late for themselves, they could at least see that their sons and daughters were better fitted for the strenuous and fervent times that were coming upon them.

For those of too high a social status to be served by Lancaster's conveyor-belt, there was a great choice of 'systems'. Most of these were descended from one potent book published in 1762, the *Émile* of Rousseau —who would certainly, however, have been very much surprised if he could have seen how most of its descen-dants turned out. He had called his method 'natural education'.

Émile, Rousseau's boy hero, was to be brought up in the country, out of doors nearly all the time, and mixing with the country people. He was to learn, so far as humanly possible, only by experience. In fact, he was to be like the aristocrats, doing what he would and taking the consequences, but without the cushioning of a privileged position. He would never be forced to do anything he did not want, never punished, nor scolded. On the other hand, if he cried without reason, he would be ignored. If he broke things, he would have to do without them. When he lost his temper, he would be treated as if he were ill. If he told lies, no one would believe anything he said. He would never, as a child, be told any stories, or be presented with anything but the naked truth. He would learn things when and because he saw that they would be of use to him. If, for instance, he did not want to learn to read, when the right time came at about eleven years of age, he would miss some attractive invitation because he could not read it. People would often refuse him what he wanted if he had nothing to offer in return and so he would acquire the idea of give and take with his fellow human beings. He would learn to put his hand to anything and discover the advantage of mastering a useful craft himself. As a young boy, he would hear nothing of art, philosophy or religion. Since a boy was not yet a rational being, said Rousseau, such things had no meaning for him. When he finally reached the age of reason, all Émile's theory would be built upon practice.

Rousseau's plan attracted considerable attention in England; but, when Richard Edgeworth, the Irish landowner and experimental philosopher, tried it on his infant son, it was not found, in this instance, to produce an amiable or convenient character. In fact, the child became quite unmanageable except by his father himself, and since his father was a lively and active person and had many other things to do, the scheme had to be abandoned. None the less, Rousseau's ideas were applied as far as possible in the bringing-up of the large Edgeworth family—or rather series of families, for Edgeworth married four times; and his eldest daughter, Maria, gave her life to the work, and became its missionary. In her hands, Rousseau's methods began to undergo a gradual transmutation into a kind of education which no one could call 'natural'.

Already, even in *Émile* itself, it had appeared too difficult in a civilised environment, always to present Émile with the simple situations which would educate him in cause and effect, and many of them had to be secretly contrived by his tutor, who must, one fears, have had to pay out quite large sums of money to induce other people to play the parts assigned to them. It was not a long step from this to the 'moral tale', in which imaginary model situations were presented, and the consequences to the child who dealt with them wisely and the child who dealt with them foolishly, strongly pointed. Many of Rousseau's disciples in France had taken to this version—or perversion—of his method, and Maria, too, found it a useful and economical supplement to the real-life experiences of her charges. A great favourite was the famous case of Little Rosamund, who, while her mother stood aside, spent her money on a purple jar from the chemist's window instead of on a pair of shoes, only to find that the colour was in the liquid, not in the glass, while the lack of the shoes led to all kinds of disappointments and disasters.

Since Maria Edgeworth lived among children, knew their ways and could speak in their idiom without the abstract words and phrases that so often stultify adult attempts to write for children, the tales were very effective and the idea that good behaviour always paid and bad behaviour did not must have been strongly impressed on her pupils, making their later experiences, one must suppose, somewhat bewildering. When the evangelical Christians adopted the method and threw the rewards and penalties of Heaven and Hell into the balance, the link with 'Nature' became even more tenuous.

One rule of Rousseau's, however, the writers of moral tales kept meticulously. There was never a touch of fantasy in their stories. The imaginary children lived in a strictly matter-of-fact world. If events fell out very pat, it was never because any magic influence intruded, but by the inexorable chain of causation in a rigidly rational universe.

'Why,' wrote Richard Edgeworth, 'should the mind be filled with fantastic visions instead of useful knowledge?' He hoped that Dr. Johnson's prestige would not avail 'to restore the reign of fairies', referring to Johnson's pronouncement, 'Babies do not want to hear about babies; they like to be told of giants and castles and of something which can stretch their little minds.' To Edgeworth, the point was not what babies wanted to hear, but what was good for them. And the Rousseau school believed that they should be confronted with reality from the beginning, and with nothing else. The evangelical writers, accepting this view, added, of course, Christian doctrines to the sum of reality.

In this spirit, Mrs. Sherwood re-edited Sarah Fielding's book for children *The Governess*, in 1817, cutting out all the fairy-tales except one, even though the original author had taken pains to emphasise that the magic was only imaginary and that the children must not let it dwell in their minds, and had provided impeccable morals. But this kind of story, Mrs. Sherwood explained, could never be generally useful, because fairy-lore could hardly be combined with Christian principle. The one exception was retained for antiquarian instruction—so that the children might see what sort of thing had amused their benighted grandparents.

The busy Mrs. Trimmer, in the meantime, established an actual censorship of children's books in her *Guardian of Education*, which ran monthly from 1802 to 1806, when it foundered among the flood of her other activities. Her favourite adjectives were 'improving' and 'exceptionable'. She expressed penitence when a correspondent pointed out that she had allowed Perrault's *Cinderella* to slip through.

> This [wrote the correspondent] is perhaps one of the most exceptionable books that was ever written for children. . . . It paints some of the worst passions that can ever enter the human heart and of which little children should, if possible, be totally ignorant; such as envy, jealousy, a dislike to mothers-in-law and half-sisters, vanity, a love of dress etc. etc.

Plays for children, Mrs. Trimmer allowed, might be written, but should never be acted. Many ill effects might follow from the assuming of fictitious characters by children and from 'throwing off the timidity which is so becoming in youth'.

Maria Edgeworth, although she was not, like Mrs. Trimmer, committed to the doctrine of original sin, does not appear to have had any such notions about children's ignorance of evil passions. In her stories, envy, jealousy, vanity, etc., appear freely, but they always bring disaster on their harbourers. Mrs. Trimmer herself sometimes takes this line, reminding one of the rules of modern American film censorship—that vice may be represented so long as it is never successful. Perhaps Cinderella would have passed muster, if she had not succeeded in marrying the prince. But the fairy godmother could never have been *persona grata* to either of the ladies.*

The Christian writers of moral tales were, of course, perturbed by Maria Edgeworth's view of reality, even while they followed her method. Jeffrey in the *Edinburgh Review* testified that 'it was impossible to read ten pages of any of her writings without feeling that not only the whole, but every part of them was intended to do good', but the religious deplored the absence of any allusion to Christianity. Maria and her father never committed themselves on this subject. When she published his memoirs, the *Quarterly Review* in vain begged her to say that he had been a Christian. The Reverend Robert Hall stigmatised the book as most pernicious because she showed 'perfect virtue without religion'.

The other side of the Rousseau-based system of education was that children should learn all possible hard facts and practical methods of dealing with them. To Rousseau, this had meant the facts important to a simple community of farmers and craftsmen and small factories. It became something different in an England undergoing the Industrial Revolution, where new inventions and discoveries were being made every day, and the country was becoming a little drunk with the sense of the scientific power that it was acquiring. Edgeworth was intensely interested in practical science; he had himself invented a new device for turning coaches more smoothly and had superintended the construction of water-works at Lyons. His house at Edgeworthstown was full of gadgets; an American author, staying there, said that the lock on her door was so complicated that she dared not use it.

*Listed among Princess Victoria's schoolbooks, besides several by Mrs. Trimmer, is one unidentified called *Poetry without Fiction* by A Mother. This suggests even a further stage of censorship.

The régime at Edgesworthstown was still near enough to Rousseau to keep a house-full of children happy, inventing, drawing plans, constructing, manipulating. At one remove, in Maria's stories, this element is almost as strong as the moral one, and presented in just the same way. Her little heroes and heroines are taken to workshops, dairies, brick-kilns and so on, and the processes carefully explained to them for their imitation. Rosamund's kind elder brother helps her to trap the rabbit that had been eating the laburnum in her little garden. It is, of course, a humane trap, which catches the culprit alive, for later release on a distant warren, and the reader is informed in a footnote in what book he can find more detailed instructions for its making.

But, in a highly complex society, the information that can be reinforced by practical experiences is too limited. What a 'naturally educated' child knew he knew well; it was a part of himself; but it was not nearly enough for a citizen of nineteenth-century Britain. Moreover, as Edgeworth himself had found, the method throws a greater strain on the educators than most of them are willing to undergo and costs more than they can afford. Émile alone had been a whole-time job for his tutor. More and more, the teachers gravitated back to books, which Rousseau had entirely ruled out for children under ten. They remained, however, books from which every imaginative stimulus had been carefully removed. The child, like Émile, learnt only facts (or what were then believed to be facts) but not only, nor even chiefly, facts that it could see and handle. Rousseau's ban on reasoning with children was also inevitably discarded when they no longer learnt only by experience.

In *The Prelude*, composed during the years 1798 to

1805, Wordsworth looked at the model child of the time and burst into lament:

> *This model of a child is never known*
> *To mix in quarrels; that were far beneath*
> *Its dignity; with gifts he bubbles o'er*
> *As generous as a fountain; selfishness*
> *May not come near him, nor the little throng*
> *Of flitting pleasures tempt him from his path . . .*
> *And natural or supernatural fear*
> *Unless it leap upon him in a dream*
> *Touches him not . . .*
>   *Not blind is he*
> *To the broad follies of the licensed world,*
> *Yet innocent himself withal, though shrewd,*
> *And can read lectures upon innocence.*
> *A miracle of scientific lore,*
> *Ships he can guide upon the pathless sea,*
> *And tell you all their cunning; he can read*
> *The inside of the earth and spell the stars,*
> *Can string you names of districts, cities, towns,*
> *The whole world over. . . .*
>   *He sifts, he weighs*
> *All things are put to question . . .*
> *For this unnatural growth the trainer blame,*
> *Pity the tree . . .*
> *For ever as a thought of purer birth*
> *Rises to lead him to a better clime,*
> *Some intermeddler still is on the watch,*
> *To drive him back and pound him like a stray,*
> *Within the pinfold of his own conceit.*
> *Meanwhile old granddam earth is sad to find*
> *The playthings which her love designed for him*
> *Unthought of; in their woodland beds the flowers*
> *Weep and the river-sides are all forlorn.*
> *Oh! give us once again the wishing-cap*
> *Of Fortunatus and the invisible coat*
> *Of Jack the Giant-Killer, Robin Hood,*
> *And Sabra in the forest with Saint George.*

Allowing for poetic exaggeration, one wonders how, even with wishing-caps and giant-killers entirely left out, the model child had been able to get all this into his time. The fierce and never-ending battle of the curriculum was in fact now beginning. Latin and Greek could still not be dispensed with; they remained the hallmarks of the ruling class. Even Brougham's clients, the knowledge-hungry working-men, sometimes showed a hankering after these talismanic accomplishments, just as, in later days, African natives disdained the agricultural and biological courses offered to them with such excellent intentions, and insisted that they must and would learn Latin. Francis Place, the brilliant background organiser of the working-class movement, describes engagingly to his wife how he is learning *amo, amas* from his friend James Mill, the economist.

But the real business of the new schooling was 'the whole circle of the sciences'. Then, too, there were modern languages, which had been added to the young gentlemen of the eighteenth century in their Grand Tours, but had to be acquired more laboriously by the new generation of pupils; there were history and political theory and political economy, all now aspiring to be regarded as sciences, and anyhow indispensable in contemporary life. The Scottish rationalists were disposed to include all these among the subjects which their children ought to study. The schools inevitably lagged behind, but began to admit more and more subjects into their time-tables. Even in Lancaster's schools, French, Geometry, Geography and Grammar soon began to be taught to such pupils as could stay the course.

The glimpse of freedom opened by Rousseau faded out for the nineteenth-century child. He could learn all that had to be learnt only by intense application to

books from the earliest possible age. Even the Edge-
worths had become convinced by the time they wrote
their *Practical Education* in 1798 that a child should
learn to read as early as possible, though they suggest
sensible methods for lightening the task.

Thomas Malkin was born in 1795 and died in 1802,
and, after his death, his father insisted on a post-
mortem, which included the dissection of the head, in
order to prove that there had been no brain disease,
because of accusations that he had pushed the child
unduly. Later, he wrote the little boy's short biography, partly from the same motive, partly from
natural grief and the desire to preserve the memory of
what was certainly a very remarkable child. Thomas
had recognised letters at eighteen months; begun to
read at two and to write at three. He could read
any English book at four. He knew the Greek
alphabet, also, and many Greek words, but was
checked at that time from going further with that
language.

The father constantly protests that all this was done
on the child's own initiative and that he was given no
encouragement; at most, only casual help. But
Thomas's own evidence hardly supports his father's
case. A precociously intelligent child is an almost irresistible temptation to elders who set a high value upon
book-learning.

'My dearest Mother,' wrote Thomas, many of whose
letters are quoted in the book, 'I was four years old
yesterday. I have got several new books; Mrs. Trimmer's *English Description; Mental Improvement* by Mrs.
Priscilla Wakefield and a Latin Grammar and English
prints.' At five, he says, 'I know a good deal of Geography
and shall be glad when I know a great deal more; for
geography, I find, is a very clever thing for me to
know.' If the poor child had used some other word—

even 'useful'—instead of that revealing 'clever', he would have done better for his father's defence.

These passages are simply written; but much of Thomas's letters are in an involved pseudo-Johnsonian style, obviously modelled on the elder Malkin's. The child often gets lost in his turgid phraseology and lapses into meaninglessness, especially when he is trying to express pious sentiments. Then he is apt to fall back upon sudden gobbets of information culled from schoolbooks, such as 'Water is, when frozen, expanded; that is, takes up more room than before'; 'The oak is a very handsome tree'; 'There is such an animal as an antelope and hippopotamus and Giraffe and Tapeir'.

Thomas wrote poems, too, but once burst into tears when pressed to do so. (His father says this was a mistake, which was never repeated.) He is a trifle hard on his younger brother, Benjamin, who was not making good progress in writing and Latin at the age of four. The father anxiously adds the comment that Benjamin is, however, very good at arithmetic and can do Rule of Three in vulgar fractions now that he is eight. Thomas, it is a relief to know, had no taste for figures.

This model child was human enough to invent an imaginary country, called Allestone, of which he made a professional-looking map, reproduced in his father's book. But the Allestonians are disappointingly dull and excessively moral people and their chief institutions are universities. 'George I', wrote Thomas, 'placed himself on the throne when he was about ten years of age, and a very proper time, too.'

Possibly, Wordsworth had Thomas Malkin in mind when he wrote his description of the model child, though the indignant surge of the verse suggests rather a vision of some local infant prodigy posing the poet with the rivers of South America or the principles of the refraction of light. Obviously, Thomas can have been typical only in the sense of being an extreme case, but he was not unique. John Stuart Mill did all that was expected of him and survived, though not quite undamaged. Such children played the part of Stakhanovite workers and raised the norm for their fellow-pupils. Fortunately, not all children are conscientious, even in a pious age. Whether the results in the case of the more dutiful ones were ever fatal can only be guessed, since such a catastrophe was not likely to be advertised. But some contemporaries clearly thought that they were. Mrs. Sherwood unexpectedly introduces into one of her moral tales a young girl of fifteen who died of overwork at school.

There is more to be said than is often said in these days for inducing a child to memorise a good deal, even of matter that it does not fully understand; since it is one of the numerous dilemmas of human nature that memory is at its best before reason and judgment have developed. In anyone who thinks at all, the information learnt in childhood falls into place in later life and supplies material for genuine reflection. However, the ideal mean between an empty and an overloaded memory has not yet been found, and probably never will be, since it must vary according to individual capacity. The eighteenth century had insisted on Latin and Greek for an educated man and left the rest to chance, environment and the intellectual appetite of the pupil. The parents of Malkin's and Mill's generation believed in cramming in everything that could by any possibility be accommodated.

Wordsworth and Charles Lamb apparently did not object so much to the sheer quantity as to the quality of the material poured into the children's minds in their times. 'Is there no possibility of averting this sore evil?' wrote Lamb to Coleridge. 'Think what you would have been now if, instead of being fed with tales and old wives' fables in childhood, you had been crammed with geography and Natural History.' Coleridge was still young, then; and few parents of any times would be anxious for their children to resemble him at a later age, great man as he was. Generally, contemporary methods, where they succeeded, produced an opposite to all that Coleridge represented— men highly self-assured, with a great respect for hard facts and practical achievement, also for such theories as they considered to have been proved, men solid in a way that their predecessors had never been, and making a strength of their earth-bound condition; and yet, in their more reflective moods, with a certain naiveté, which sometimes has an aroma of wistfulness.

THE EMERGENCE OF THE PERFECT LADY

Be good, sweet maid and let who can be clever.
CHARLES KINGSLEY

WHILE the young of the early nineteenth century were expected to assimilate large quantities of miscellaneous information, there were other things that they were expected carefully to avoid knowing; and, if their elders could forget them, too, so much the better. There exists an excellent diet sheet to illustrate the state of mental digestion in the reading public of the time. This is Bowdler's *Family Shakespeare*.

In this version of the national dramatist, according to the foreword, 'nothing is added to the original text; but those words and expressions are omitted which cannot with propriety be read in a family'. This claim is not strictly correct; not merely words and expressions, but whole passages which offend the editor's taste or which, he presumes, would offend the family's taste, are cut and, on the other hand, lines which have been mutilated in this process are filled out to make the verse run smoothly. On the whole, Bowdler did this latter task competently; needless to say, he adds no beauties to Shakespeare, but his small interpolations are not often painfully conspicuous. He was indeed a man of education and culture, a doctor, a fellow of the Royal Society and of the Society of Antiquaries. He had been a member of Mrs. Montagu's coterie in the seventeen-eighties. He was also one of the earliest members of the Society for the Suppression of Vice and a friend of Wilberforce.

Bowdler's alterations of Shakespeare's text fall into two distinct classes—those made in deference to religious prejudice, and those made in the interests of decency and delicacy.

Twelfth Night, one of the most familiar of the plays, may be taken as typical. God must never be mentioned, whether the use of the name is frivolous or serious. 'Excellently done,' says Viola about Olivia's complexion, 'if God did all.' In Bowdler's version this becomes 'If Nature did all'. 'Nature' or 'Heaven', according to the context, usually do duty for 'God'. Or the nurse in *Romeo and Juliet* must say 'Susan's dead' instead of 'Susan is with God'. Olivia and the Fool are not permitted their dialogue about her dead brother, concluding with the line, 'The more fool, Madonna, to mourn for your brother's soul being in Heaven.' This subtle criticism of the genuineness of Christians' beliefs could evidently not be stomached. Nor may the love-sick Olivia say, 'A fiend like thee might bear my soul to hell.' Clergymen are also sacred. When the Fool puts on the parson's gown, he must not say, 'And would I were the first that ever dissembled in such a gown.'

Apart from the obvious omissions for indecency—*Measure for Measure* is cut by an eighth and Doll Tearsheet entirely eliminated from *Henry IV*—none of the grosser physical functions may be alluded to. Even the mild 'I know my physic will work with him' is cut. When the lines about women are omitted:

> *Alas, their love may be called appetite,*
> *No motion of the liver, but the palate,*
> *That suffer surfeit, cloyment and revolt,*

one wonders whether the objection is to the attribution of sensuality to women or to the unpleasant suggestion of vomiting; but, as the opening lines of the play, which, for all their mellifluous sound, make a similar suggestion, are left untouched, it is probably faith in the spiritual nature of feminine love that the censor is safeguarding. This view is confirmed by the cutting of the dialogue about Viola's potential beard, so that she is saved the immodesty of saying, 'By my troth, I'll tell thee, I am almost sick for one, though I would not have it grow upon my chin.' The word 'body' itself is generally replaced by 'person', though, when Hamlet refers to 'lugging' Polonius' 'guts', 'body' is allowed to represent this greater grossness. After all, 'person' would hardly describe a corpse.

Before *Othello*, Bowdler frankly capitulates. Admitting that the play is 'one of the noblest efforts of dramatic art', the subject, he says, is 'unfortunately little suited to family reading'. It is impossible to purge it of indecent expressions without altering Othello's character—in fact, destroying the tragedy. In this dilemma, Shakespeare wins. Because the play is calculated to produce 'an excellent effect on the human mind' as a warning against jealousy, and moreover inculcates the Christian and rational view that 'adultery is a crime next to murder', Bowdler has refrained from omissions that would destroy its force. He advises that, if his version is not thought sufficiently 'correct' for family reading, it shall be transferred 'from the parlour to the cabinet'.

Bowdler did not confine himself to Shakespeare. He 'bowdlerised' also Gibbon's *Decline and Fall of the Roman Empire*, omitting altogether the famous fourteenth and fifteenth chapters with their cool, ironic account of early Christianity. There is perhaps a faintly sinister ring in his claim that, if Gibbon could now make his wishes known, he would 'desire nothing more ardently' than that this new version of his work should represent him to posterity.

Certainly, as his nephew claimed after Bowdler's death, it had been his 'peculiar happiness' to have so rendered Shakespeare and Gibbon that 'they could no longer raise a blush on the cheek of modest innocence, nor plant a pang in the heart of the devoutest Christian'. By this time, it is clear that modest innocence could no longer endure the word 'body' (unless dead) and that devout Christians could no longer admit that there were parsons capable of guile.

Bowdler's Shakespeare first appeared in 1804. By 1818, there had been six editions and it continued to be republished at intervals throughout the century. There was a new edition as late as 1896. In 1807 it was reviewed by the *British Critic*, a Tory review, which was disdainful about it, supposing that 'there are doubtless squeamish people to whom these mutilations will be acceptable', but that, though some Elizabethan dramatists might be better expurgated, 'Shakespeare, we should think, might have escaped.' After all, 1807 was a somewhat early date in the revolution of taste, and one may surmise that the first readers were confined to the earlier Evangelical converts. But by 1820 the *Edinburgh Review*, in spite of its progressiveness, strongly approved, and thought that Bowdler's ought to become the standard Shakespeare, not only for the drawing-room, but for the closet, since 'it is better every way that what cannot be spoken, and ought not to have been written, should now cease to be printed'.

This was more than Bowdler himself had claimed. He intended his Shakespeare for reading aloud in the family circle, a very general custom at the time. He evidently did not imagine that it would do himself any harm to study the original text, and he expected the father of the family to read *Othello* and the other unexpurgated plays in his own sanctum. It was the young people and the modest innocence of the female members of the household that were to be protected against the full impact of Shakespeare. Yet Bowdler, as a member of the Blue-Stocking circle, must often in his youth have met Johnson, one of the devoutest Christians of his day, who once scolded a mother for giving her young daughter only books of a moral tendency, suitable to her youth: 'Then you are a fool, Madam. Turn your daughter loose into your library; if she is well inclined, she will only choose nutritious food; if otherwise, all your precautions will avail nothing to prevent her following the natural bent of her inclinations.'

Johnson, however, was at least partly wrong. He was thinking of his own kind. Those excepted, a great deal can be done by keeping people in ignorance. Some will, of course, break out, but not the majority. As Wilberforce had always believed, while external restrictions cannot alter the fundamental nature of a human being, they can control its outward manifestations; and, if the next generation of growing boys and girls do not see, nor hear of, some possibilities, the odds are that they will never think of them. We have reason to know this in our own day, for it is what is happening in the curtained-off portion of the world.

Bowdler was by no means the most prudish of his contemporaries. Leigh Hunt gives the history of the translation of an old French romance in which a Knight, accused of cowardice, fights and conquers three opponents while wearing in place of armour his lady's vest, which she has scornfully sent him instead of the favour he had asked for. The first title of the poem in English was *The Three Knights and the Smock*. Then 'smock' became indelicate and the title was altered to *The Three Knights and the Shift*. Then the article was thought less offensive in its French form, *The Three Knights and the Chemise*. Now, says Hunt, that word may not be mentioned at all, nor the garment itself alluded to by any decent writer. Ultimately, the whole poem was withdrawn. Hunt, something of an *enfant terrible* in his generation, found the public 'people of unaccountable imagination'.

Writers of the older generation who had their livings to earn found it desirable to conform. Southey, who has not kept the moral respect of posterity to the extent that he enjoyed that of his contemporaries, goes to surprising lengths in his biography of Nelson. There is no reason to believe, he says, that the hero's unfortunate attachment to Lady Hamilton was 'criminal'. Thomas Moore was more dignified in his deference to popular standards. His Lives of Byron, of whom he was an intimate friend, and of Sheridan, make no such positive statements. They merely omit.

The two strains in Bowdler's censorship, that of piety and that of prudishness, were, after all, connected and the link was St. Paul. In accepting the Bible as a complete rule of life, the Evangelicals accepted St. Paul's views about the rôle of women implicitly :

> In like manner also that women adorn themselves in modest apparel, with shamefacedness and sobriety, not with broided hair, or gold or pearls or costly array.
> But (which becometh women professing godliness) with good works.
> Let the woman learn in silence and with all subjection.
> But I suffer not a woman to teach, nor to usurp authority over the man, but to be in silence.

Hannah More, changeling child of the Blue-Stockings, though she can hardly have taken the injunction about teaching quite literally, did not shrink from this programme. On the contrary, she had what Roman Catholics would call a special devotion to St. Paul, and wrote a book on his character and writings. When this was published in 1815, there were still numerous and vocal rebels among her sex, and she takes pains to defend him against their attack. How can it be supposed, she asks with somewhat superficial psychology, that a man who had so many valued women friends had an antagonism to women? He was merely showing them their proper rôle and she would be sorry to think they wished to oppose his view 'that she that liveth in pleasure is dead while she liveth'.

Good works were now becoming almost the only outlet left to women under the evangelical dispensation, and even these had to be on a strictly private basis. Wilberforce would not allow them to take any public part even in the Anti-Slavery agitation. It might lead, he said, to other political intrusions, 'unsuited to the female character as delineated in Scripture'. There are extraordinarily few allusions to his own wife in his biography by his sons, apart from one serious illness. Her health is inquired after by correspondents, and she is mentioned once or twice as disliking social functions and being of a retiring disposition. His affection for her is taken for granted, but she was evidently not of a type to modify his ideas of the female character.

In these circumstances, the emergence of the Blue-Stockings in the later eighteenth century, discreet as it was, turned out to have no future.* 'Propriety' closed firmly in on the next generation of women. Mrs. Montagu, the 'Queen of the Blues', had objected to

* The solitary extremist rebel of the late eighteenth century, Mary Wollstonecraft, was so untypical that she hardly affects a study of general social development.

the scenes in which Doll Tearsheet figured, as Bowdler claimed in his preface to *Henry IV*, but she would certainly have found his aversion to the word 'body' very funny, while the refusal of Hannah More to accept membership of the Royal Society of Literature on grounds of feminine modesty, could only have appalled the pioneer who had tried to promote the foundation of a college for the higher education of women.

In this closing circle, the course of the one woman of genius living in England at the time makes a little comedy of which she was probably aware, but which she was unfortunately not in a position to exploit. Jane Austen was twenty-five years firmly rooted in the eighteenth century. On the other hand, she was daughter and sister of clergymen and had, quite willingly, to do the proper thing. Limitations do not seem to have worried her; having genius, she made an asset of them, so that her stories gain by their closed, cosy little circles of family life with their narrow bounds of thought and behaviour. Even so, certain revisions appear in the later editions of her novels, which show the slow pressure of public opinion. In the second edition of *Sense and Sensibility* a mention of 'a natural son' is deleted, and evasive action is taken in a similar situation in *Emma*. Lydia in *Pride and Prejudice* comes well out of her elopement, unblessed by the Church, but, in the later novels, no culprit of this kind escapes sharp punishment. In accordance with Bishop Porteus' prescription, Maria Bertram in *Mansfield Park* is sent into austere retirement for life.

The evangelical wave really shook Jane Austen about the time of its culminating force around 1810–20. It was the campaign to make clergymen not merely more dutiful, but more respected that caught her. It could hardly be otherwise, since her life was as domestic as her books, and her family was clerical. In *Coelebs* *in Search of a Wife*, published in 1809, Hannah More had blamed novelists for their detrimental portraits of clergymen. Even when they were shown as good men, she said, they were given ridiculous traits. This was wrong; it undermined their influence. Whether clergymen, being human beings, in fact had such traits, was of no importance to her, and her own clergymen were accordingly puppets. Jane Austen evidently regarded Hannah More's work a trifle pettishly. When *Coelebs* appeared, she felt disinclined to read it. 'I do not like Evangelicals,' she wrote. 'Of course, I shall be delighted when I read it like other people.' * But she must have been affected by the criticism of novelists' portraits of clergymen, especially when it was applied to her Rev. Mr. Collins in *Pride and Prejudice*, which, though not published until 1813, was written long before. Her next clergyman was of a very different type —the almost immaculate Edmund Bertram of *Mansfield Park*, who gave up the woman he loved because she wanted him to be an absentee parson. About the same time, Jane Austen was strongly advising her niece not to reject an otherwise eligible suitor because 'his religious views eventually induced him to think that dancing and other social amusements ought to be eschewed and avoided by Christian people'; and she goes so far as to add, 'I am by no means convinced that we ought not all to be evangelical and am at least persuaded that they who are so from reason and feeling must be happiest and safest.' The keyword here is perhaps 'safest'. The good aunt, no doubt anxious to see a somewhat flighty niece securely settled, may well have stretched her own sentiments a little.† However

* This, however, is incredible.
† One realises in reading Jane Austen's letters, that, unlike many authors, she never had any idea of their being published, which is perhaps why some readers find them disappointing.

that may be, it is reassuring to find that Jane Austen continued to go to the theatre and could still create in *Emma* a clergyman who is certainly no improvement on Mr. Collins.

Because Jane Austen's comments on the life around her were those of art, she has been criticised for ignoring the great historical changes that were going on in her lifetime. It is true that her novels contain no direct comment on the Napoleonic wars; yet the closing paragraph of *Persuasion* could have been written only by a woman who had lived through a war. Nor had she anything to say about the Industrial Revolution. But then the Industrial Revolution is more significant to us, because it has produced us, than it ever appeared to the society that inaugurated it. Great stress is laid by modern historians on the movements and the sufferings of factory workers in the early nineteenth century, but they are, in fact, talking of what was then a small minority. Around 1815, only a fifth of the inhabitants of Great Britain lived in towns of over 50,000. The norm was still country life ; and Jane Austen was nothing if not normal.*

About the changes in social habits and manners, apart from the Evangelical movement, she had plenty to say—by implication. Mrs. Radcliffe's version of the romantic mood inspired the farce of *Northanger Abbey*; and what Jane Austen thought of the learned child may be inferred from the conversations of Mary Bennett with her cruel father, a scholar of the old type.

Most people associate Jane Austen with 'propriety', but her propriety was still nearer to the common-sense propriety of the eighteenth century than to the new prudish propriety of the nineteenth. Miss Bingley won

* No less exceptional for that, of course, normal minds being as rare as normal eyesight.

no victory when she tried to belittle Elizabeth Bennett to Darcy.

> To walk three miles, or four miles, or five miles, or whatever it is, above her ankles in the dirt, and alone, quite alone! What could she mean by it? It seems to show an abominable sort of conceited independence, a most country-town indifference to decorum. . . . Endeavour to check that little something, bordering on conceit and impertinence, which your lady possesses.

Yet, in 1814, there was at least one woman reader, and not an insignificant one, to agree with Miss Bingley. It is startling to find Jane Austen accused by a distinguished fellow-author of an 'entire want of taste' in producing 'so pert, so worldly a heroine as the beloved of such a man as Darcy'. Mary Mitford makes confusion worse confounded by adding, 'Wickham is equally bad.' As the turning-point of the plot of *Pride and Prejudice* is Wickham's badness, this can only mean that it was bad taste to have him in the book at all. None the less, Mary Mitford had the discrimination to prefer Jane Austen to Maria Edgeworth. She continues:

> If the former had a little more taste, a little more perception of the graceful, as well as of the humorous, I know not indeed anyone to whom I should not prefer her. There is none of the hardness, the cold selfishness of Edgeworth about her writings; she is in a much better humour with the world; she preaches no sermons; she wants nothing but the *beau ideal* of the female character, to be a perfect novel-writer.

However, it never becomes quite clear what Mary Mitford's *beau ideal* of the female character was. She was twelve years younger than Jane Austen, having

been born in the crucial year of 1787—the year of the
Proclamation and the beginning of Wilberforce's crusade. She thus belonged to the generation of bewildered boys and girls caught between the standards,
morals and tastes of the Age of Reason and those of the
Victorian Age. Unlike Jane Austen, she was the studi-
ous type of girl, and was often called a Blue-Stocking.
From the evidence of her letters and diaries one can
only conclude that the transition was almost as confusing and uncomfortable for an intellectual woman as
the emotional struggles of a Harriet Cavendish or a
Caroline Lamb.

Mary Mitford had, however, considerable excuse
for muddle-headedness. She was peculiarly unfortunate in her father, a fascinating waster of good family,
who ran through 'six or seven fortunes' at record speed.
She had had a happy and somewhat pampered childhood and her bookish habits were certainly her own
choice. She once, in her teens, she says, read fifty
books in one month. This was not because the school
where she finished her education was of the new kind,
calculated to produce learned children. On the contrary, it was run by a French emigré, M. St. Quentin,
and specialised in the graces. As Mary Butt also went
there a few years earlier, we know a good deal about
it. The girls were taught music, dancing—even, in
Mary Mitford's time, the waltz, then still a daring
innovation, which she calls 'un-English'—needlework,
elegant handwriting, French and English. They were
even allowed to act a play. However, the new ideals
must have been having some effect, even here, in
1800, for

this play was not anything that could, by any
possibility, inoculate our young imaginations with a
love of the stage and its wit and vanity. No . . . our

performance was one which could never by any chance produce such an effect; it was neither more nor less than Miss Hannah More's dramatic homily, *The Search after Happiness*, and was designed equally to mend our morals and improve our declamation. All our actresses, the indolent, the romantic and the vain, were fitted with parts which touched their respective foibles.

In such a performance, even Mrs. Trimmer could hardly have seen serious harm.

As the above quotations show, such crude propaganda had little effect on one youthful mind at least. Mary Mitford's environment as a girl was free and pleasant in the old style. After school, which she left at fifteen, there were a few more years of gaiety and visiting and dancing until 5 a.m. The family politics were Whig, verging on Radical, and her early hero was Fox, later to be replaced by Cobbett. Dr. Mitford was as easy-going with his daughter as with himself, while Mary's Victorian biographer remarks, with pained surprise, that her mother's letters to her at school were full of chit-chat without a word of advice, moral or religious. He concludes that she must have relied entirely upon example.

From this early freedom, Mary Mitford grew up to violent vicissitudes of wealth and poverty and to constant worry over the behaviour of her much loved but irresponsible father, who had to be forestalled in his attempts to borrow on the Trust Fund which became their only reliable source of income, and to be followed and fetched back from his excursions to the gambling tables of London. Finally, when she was still quite young, she had to turn the talent for writing which had hitherto given her nothing but pleasure to the slavish labour of supporting both parents for the rest of their lives, with no brother or sister to share the burden.

Dr. Mitford, as is common in his care-free type, lived on into old age, long surviving his wife, and was again in danger of arrest for debt in the last year of his life. His daughter was fifty-five when he died, and the degree of her exhaustion is measured by the fact that she wrote no more for eight years.

It is not surprising that, in this harassed existence, Mary Mitford never seems to have had time to think or sort her ideas into any kind of consistency. Like most authors compelled to write too much, she wrote with great prolixity, and probably never revised anything not for immediate publication. Her editor groans over the frightful labour of deciphering her hasty illegible scribble. But what they lose in lucidity, her letters and diaries gain as social evidence. They present an incessant mental seesaw between the wide and the narrow outlook, between good and vulgarised taste. In her work for publication, her wretched domestic situation forced her to be a journalistic writer. She had to produce what was wanted, with a constant eye to the money it must bring in. And public taste was all set for moral improvement, gentility and feminine delicacy. This pressure seems gradually to have modified her own views, so that the robust, somewhat self-assertive young woman of intellect and the refined, dependent female who loved flowers and abhorred everything coarse fought in her all her life and were never reconciled.

'In this educating age,' she wrote at twenty-five in 1812, 'everything is taught to women except that which is perhaps worth all the rest—the power and habit of thinking,' and she boldly characterised her father's radical associates as 'your canting friends' and 'canting Scotchmen'. Yet in 1815 came the prize ode, *The March of Mind*, celebrating the anniversary of Brougham's 'British and Foreign Schools Society', whose most remarkable stanza has already been quoted:

> *Instruction, child of Heaven and Earth,*
> *As heat expands the vernal flower*
> *So wisdom, goodness, freedom, power,*
> *From thee derive their birth.*

Similarly, though she found *Ossian* 'more mawkish than a modern tragedy', it was just this kind of romantic tragedy that largely enabled her to maintain her parents and her home for twenty years.

These plays were as much pot-boilers as her books. She canvassed her friends for plots on historical and romantic themes—not too recent or conspicuous, because then they would have to be accurate. She records, too, that she wrote seven endings to her play, *Foscari*, so that Macready might choose the one he preferred. In this play, she treated the same subject as Byron—one of the favourite Italian Renaissance plots of the time, replete with intrigue, treachery and political murder. Neither is a good play. Mary's is naturally less eloquent, but would as certainly act better, even though she avoids the physical torture in which Byron revels.*

None of Mary Mitford's plays was a comedy. Even in her early unregenerate days, Hannah More, too, had produced nothing but tragedies, a fact which her pious biographer mentions as if it were some slight extenuation. In Mary Mitford, this bias can hardly have been spontaneous, for the principle charm of her other work is its humour, and, as time went on, she

* Modern playgoers, however, are never likely to have an opportunity to judge for themselves, for not a single play of the period has passed into the English Classical repertory. If it had not, paradoxically, at the same time, produced a series of fine actors, the English theatre could hardly have survived the evangelical attack.

began to show a misgiving that, even in tragedy, play-writing was not altogether a fitting activity for her sex, exclaiming against the 'unwomanly publicity' in which it involved her. She would rather, she says, serve in a shop, rather scour floors—rather nurse children. But some of this must be the reaction normal to dramatists of any period in the agony of seeing their brain children mangled by producers and actors, for, a year or two later, she confesses to a preference for play-writing; the 'unwomanly' is evidently yet another tribute to invading convention. After her, there were no more women dramatists of any note, tragic or comic, until the nineteenth century was nearing its close.

On the other hand, her connection with the stage must have helped to fortify Mary Mitford against evangelical pressure, since she could not, even if she had wished, have afforded to give it up. She never succumbed to the religious wave as an individual, confessing to a clerical friend in middle life that she could not believe all that the Church required, though she claimed 'a devout sense of the mercy of God'. A 'very great lady' once attempted to convert her to Methodism, but was successfully evaded. Such pursuits were even more common now than when Wilberforce and his early band of devotees had set about the conversion of their fellow-citizens. Even Lady Byron, pious herself, once gave refuge to a Lady Gosford, fleeing from her formidable sister-in-law, Lady Olivia Sparrow, a friend of Hannah More's, who was determined to convert her. Mary Mitford described her difficulty once in extricating a feeble old friend from an evangelical service which had already lasted two and a half hours. Privately, she often stood out against the excesses of the new Puritanism. She would never admit that punishment and misfortune were good for people, though that was 'the prevailing sentiment'. She objected to Miss Hawkins's 'sermonising' novels, especially *The Countess and Gertrude*, which advocated 'a rigorous discipline in youth in order to prepare for the misfortunes of old age'.

But it was one thing to resist direct conversion, and another to escape the wave of Pauline prudishness in which she had to work and earn her living. Mary put up something of a fight—again privately—over Byron's case.

She admired his poetry and was overcome by the pathos of his farewell to his country. Certainly, at a later stage, she became 'rather sick of all that sublimity' and 'being made one of 100,000 confidants of his lordship's mysterious and secret sorrows'. But she was impatient of the chorus of condolence for Lady Byron.

> Why did she marry him? for, to do the man justice, he was no hypocrite, his vices were public enough, Why did she marry him but to partake his celebrity and bask in the sunshine of his fame? . . . She has now the comfort of being interesting in the eyes of all men and 'exemplary' in the mouths of all women.

This was actually unfair to Annabella Byron, but reasonable enough on the facts known, and certainly not mawkish. In Mary's final judgment of Byron's work after his death, the moral bias returns. 'But the want of purity! God forbid that I should be a canter, but the want of purity—the harm that both he and Mr. Moore have done to the young men and women of the day—must not be overlooked, though I trust it is forgiven.'

This 'God forbid that I should be a canter' is probably the nearest Mary Mitford ever came to recognising the conflict of standards in her own mind. As her life and her struggles for livelihood progressed, her preference for sheltered virtue and shrinking refinement increased. A projected book of her own was 'to be free from vice and pecuniary evil (both of which are so unpleasant in books)' and its conclusion 'comfortable and satisfactory'. The bias against 'pecuniary evil' is very understandable in her circumstances; but it does not seem to have occurred to this bookworm to wonder how many books would have been left for her sustenance if both these forms of unpleasantness had been cut out. However, the preference for 'favour and prettiness' was not entirely a matter of taste, as is evident from her advice to her young friend, Elizabeth Barrett, the future Mrs. Browning, to give her stories happy endings in order to sell. This is necessary, she says, even for cultivated readers.

Reading *Pickwick Papers* towards the end of her life, Mary Mitford approved because 'a lady might read it all aloud', but (eighteenth-century standards flickering again) being 'fidgety about style' and so expecting books to be written in English, she could not read his more serious passages. The old English dramatists must have been deeply rooted in her youthful affections, for she still thought them the best reading of all, 'of course admitting and regretting the coarseness of the age', which 'one skips'. She does not say whether she made use of Bowdler in reading Shakespeare. Probably not, since, with all this daintiness, she never abandoned her claim to intellectual independence and would still prefer to do her own censoring.

It is clear that in Mary Mitford the 'perfect lady' of the Victorian Age was emerging. The coarser aspects of life are to be kept out of sight. 'One skips them.' It is so even in *Our Village*, her masterpiece, with its lovely, chaste, classical style. In this village, there are rags and

poverty sometimes, but only to be relieved by generosity; there are peccadilloes and follies, but never crime,
nor vice; and the proportion of good-looking, intelligent and happy people is enough to create a Utopia.
One ends by longing for a little roughness and ugliness. American admirers, coming in search of this
idyllic scene, were abashed to find a harassed, overworked woman to whom their visits were an obvious
embarrassment.

Mary was certainly justified when she asked a clerical
friend if she might dedicate to him one of her rural
series. She would never, she says, suggest dedicating a
play to him for fear of harming him in his profession,
but even those who do not allow novels in the house,
sanction her little books. This request was made in
1837, the year of Victoria's accession, and seems to
show the Evangelicals' work in this sphere completed.

Most people of her generation did not become so
confused as Mary Mitford over the change in taste
through which they were passing, because most people
are even less aware of what is happening to them than
she was. There is a curious story of an old lady in
Lockhart's *Life of Scott*. She asked Scott to obtain for
her Aphra Behn's novels, which she had so much enjoyed in her youth. With some misgiving, he complied,
only to have them returned with a request to put them
on the fire. She had not been able to read through
even one of them. 'But is it not a very odd thing', she
wrote, 'that I, an old woman of eighty and upwards,
sitting alone, feel ashamed to read a book which, sixty
years ago, I have heard read aloud for the amusement
of large circles, consisting of the first and most credit-
able society in London?'

It is odd, but not unusual. In our own times, Henry
James has become unreadable to many, not because of
his obscurity, but because he usually confined himself

to the class of people who were alone in a position to nourish the subtleties of feeling in which he was interested.

How many of the 'perfect ladies' of the Victorian era might have become something more exhilarating, we shall never know. But human nature is like an air-balloon. If you depress it in one place, it bulges in another. The few Victorian women who did succeed in extricating themselves from their narrow environment acquired so much character in the process, that they became Juggernauts. Charity was the only outlet left to them, apart from the writing of refined novels; but it is not always easy to restrain charity from expanding into public philanthropy. Harriet Martineau, who was born just when Mary Mitford was leaving school, combined with a moral earnestness that eclipsed all her male contemporaries, a determination that sex should not bar anyone from putting principles into practice on the widest scale. When Americans told her that the Abolitionists were unsexing women in using them in their political campaign, so that good men found it necessary to republish in the United States good little English books on woman's appropriate moral sphere, she asked:

'But what is her appropriate moral sphere?'

'Why, certainly a special and different one from Man's.'

'But, if so, she would have had a special and different Christ.'

'But dear Miss Martineau, is it possible you think women have the same duties and rights as men?'

'I think their powers ought to settle that question.'

For herself, her powers did settle it. Ultimately, cabinet ministers hung on the publication of her pamphlets and the most assured social oracle turned pale when her ear-trumpet was directed at him. Her younger friend, Florence Nightingale, of whom Mary Mitford, by that time an old lady, strongly disapproved, was another who made governments tremble. And there were Annie Besant and Emmeline Pankhurst still to come. One and all, including the Queen herself, contrived to make a weapon of their very Victorian womanliness, before which men had to lower their own weapons in shame and reverence, or incur general obliquy if they did not.

Pauline restrictions may have suppressed many, but they ensured also that the outstanding women of the Victorian Age should be women of ferocious goodness and devastating strength of purpose.

'THE MOST ENLIGHTENED GENERATION'

No doubt but ye are the people and wisdom shall die with you.

JOB, xii. 2

WRITING in 1830, young Thomas Macaulay, who had been born at the turn of the century, referred to his contemporaries almost casually, in a subordinate clause, as 'the most enlightened generation of the most enlightened people that ever existed'.

The young people of whom he was talking had, most of them, grown up free of the doubt and confusion that had worried those who were by some fifteen years their elders. They knew right from wrong, and they knew that they were better than their parents. They were conscious of no deprivation.

No one had a stronger claim than Macaulay himself to be regarded as the child of the social regeneration. 'Of the strictest sect of our religion', he quoted St. Paul in later life, 'I was bred a Pharisee.' His father had been one of Wilberforce's closest colleagues in the Slave Trade campaign, and was a rigid Evangelical, to whom, as his grandson said, 'Nature had denied any sense of the ridiculous.' Macaulay's mother had been a pupil of Hannah More. Hannah herself he acknowledged as a second mother, having paid many a visit to her home at Barley Wood during his childhood.

It happened, however, that this child of the Pharisees was gifted with a powerful intellect. This—a not

entirely comfortable endowment in pre-Victorian days
—gives to his career among the new taboos a peculiar
interest. His father Zachary, in a sense which he would
not have recognised, may have been Macaulay's salvation, since such a father ensured an antagonistic
reaction in a son of lively intelligence. The sons of
Wilberforce never lapsed from his ideals during their
father's lifetime. Macaulay, since a transfer from one
enthusiasm to another was almost the only switch
possible to a young intellectual at his time and in his
circumstances, passed to the other camp of zealots, the
offspring of the Scottish school. Here, he was able to
develop wider views and less regimented tastes than
would have been possible among the Saints, though
hardly a blander attitude of mind.

As usual among the Evangelicals, public schools
were rejected for Macaulay's education. From the age
of twelve he went to a small private school run by a
clergyman. Here, says Sir G. O. Trevelyan, Macaulay's nephew and biographer:

> Theological topics dragged into the conversation
> at unexpected moments, inquiries about their spiri-
> tual state and long sermons which had to be listened
> to under the dire obligation of reproducing them
> in an epitome, fostered in the minds of some boys
> a reaction against the outward manifestations of
> religion—a reaction which had already begun under
> the strict system pursued in their respective homes.

On Sundays, the boys went to Church twice, learnt a
chapter of the Greek Testament, and wrote out the
sermon after tea; 'otherwise, it was a day of rest'.
Trevelyan does not say expressly that Macaulay was
one of the boys who reacted against this régime; but
it seems a fair inference.

The teaching at this school was still of the public

school type, almost (apart from religious instruction) confined to the classics, with nothing of the scientific lore fostered by Brougham and his friends. But it seems to have followed the fashion in demanding intense industry of its pupils. However, Macaulay was obviously one of those children who, in any circumstances, will race ahead of whatever education may be imposed upon them. He is said to have begun reading at the age of three and was always mentally omnivorous. One of his first recorded clashes with his father was on the question of 'idle reading'. The family compromised by reading novels, but never in the morning, and Zachary allowed this to pass, though he continued to disapprove. Reading between the lines of the biographer, who, as a member of the family, must have been under some constraint, one can easily see that the exuberant boy led the younger members of the family in rebellion against the rigidity of their parents and that his mental gymnastics continually baffled them.

One intellectual prank of young Macaulay's carried on the light reading controversy. Zachary was now editor of the *Christian Observer*, the paper for which Wilberforce had expressed fears in 1802, lest its heaviness should sink it. In 1816 Zachary's sixteen-year-old son contrived to have inserted in it a letter signed 'Candidus' in defence of novel-reading. As an earlier correspondent had written against this 'dangerous amusement', he had his pretext. Macaulay's letter was extremely orthodox, not to say priggish, basing its argument on the moral good that could be drawn from novels judiciously selected. It managed to slip in, however, a good word even for Fielding and Smollett; and a hornets' nest began to buzz about the unlucky editor's ears. A letter from 'Northern Vicar' was too candid even to quote. He did not himself, Zachary protested, agree with the contentions of 'Candidus', he merely thought that the practice of novel-reading was so widespread that it ought to be discussed— which suggests the line of argument his son must have used to get his opportunity. The controversy ran on through the year, in mainly hostile letters, though the enemy was a little embarrassed by the impossibility of condemning Hannah More's *Coelebs*, which Macaulay had used adroitly in the original letter. The incident was, in effect, a rehearsal for a curious, unacknowledged debate between the moralist and the æsthete that continued in Macaulay's mind to the end of his days.

At Cambridge, Macaulay was converted to near-Radicalism by a fellow-undergraduate, to the consternation of his family; but he later and permanently settled down as a zealous Whig reformer. It must have been highly satisfactory to him when the main bodies of the two sections fused in the Reform Bill agitation of the early thirties, giving rise to the new Liberal party. In this evolution, he shed the peculiar stigmata of the Evangelical—the exclusive devotion of Sunday to religious exercises, condemnation of the theatre and so on. What he could not discard was their intense preoccupation with morality, and for him Liberal principles were added to the sum of morality.

A fanatic for liberal principles is in a curious position. He cannot, as an enthusiast for freedom of speech, freedom of the Press and freedom of enterprise, advocate, like the Society for the Suppression of Vice, that everything he disapproves of should be stopped by law. But, for Macaulay, it did not follow that one need show anything beyond a purely legal tolerance for other people's views. Even in that positive and complacent generation of intellectuals—Thomas Arnold, Harriet Martineau, Carlyle, John Stuart Mill, all seeing themselves as preachers, teachers and guardians of innocence, were about Macaulay's age—found his self-confidence and assertiveness alarming, while that belated eighteenth-century aristocrat, Lord Melbourne, only wished that he were as certain of anything as that young man was of everything.

Macaulay's life was one of transparent honesty in all his outward dealings, combined with the pathetic faith of the Scottish school in the power of rationality. The men of the Age of Reason had sometimes also shown this childish confidence in the power of argument to alter people for the better; hence Lord Chesterfield's impassioned reasoning with his son in his efforts to make a fine gentleman of him. But they had not thought to apply such methods to the management of the people at large; their sense of reality had been too strong for that. As Lord Chesterfield himself had remarked to the House of Lords, 'A free people must be treated like a fine woman. If she has now and then a little caprice, you must not flatly contradict her. You must give way, or at least seem to give way, to her humour; till, by good treatment and a delicate opposition, you find an opportunity to give a turn to her temper.' Macaulay, standing as candidate for Leeds, condemned all canvassing on high moral and rational principles. It was as much to the interest of the electors, he said, to choose a good representative as it was to his interest to be chosen. A candidate should state his opinions, but give no pledges, since he is an expert in politics and the electors are not. 'It is not necessary to my happiness that I should sit in Parliament,' he wrote, 'but it is necessary to my happiness that I should possess, in Parliament or out of it, the consciousness of having done what is right.'

In the Leeds election, in the enthusiasm following

the passage of the Reform Bill, the method succeeded.
It did not succeed so well throughout his political
career. Macaulay's ability was so conspicuous that he
was quickly in office, but he never reached high office.
He was an impracticable colleague, frequently suffer-
ing from scruples at awkward moments. Later, his
Edinburgh constituents threw him over in a fit of impatience. He harangued their deputations, they said,
instead of listening to them; he did not answer their
letters and neglected their requests; he was so determined to be independent and disinterested that he
would not even subscribe to the 'race-cup'. Later they
repented, but, by that time, his health was already
declining and he had long before decided that literature was his true vocation. Macaulay's relations with
his constituents make a curious contrast with those of
Wilberforce, who had been just as drastic in insisting
on his principles, but had been bred in a courteous
age, apart from his mild and friendly temperament.

All this fierce independence is the more remarkable
in that Macaulay's father had lost most of his money
when his son was still an undergraduate, and the son
was soon obliged to become the main support of the
family. Sheer ability enabled him to do it in spite of
his intransigence—that and the fact that his ideas
were, after all, in the main current of the movement
of the times.

It is in his writings only that an underlying discomfort in Macaulay betrays itself. The conduct of his life
would stand the closest scrutiny of the most strait-
laced Victorian moralist. It would almost seem that
he was never even tempted by any wanton spirit, for
his moral consistency was protected by an almost complete lack of æsthetic sensibility. He valued art and
architecture only for their historic interest. He had no
ear for music. The graces of life were indifferent to

him. He used conversation to give and receive ideas and opinions—especially to give them—and was shunned by those who still had any conception of conversation as an art. He dressed, says his biographer, 'badly, but not cheaply'. He was very little concerned with what he ate, though he liked to entertain generously. He was physically clumsy, useless and uninterested in any form of sport. His only exercise was walking, often with a book in his hand.

Yet there remained one entry for the seducer—that particular æsthetic sensibility which is most widespread and which few, if any, human beings lack completely—the sense of drama. Macaulay had this in so high a degree that, in spite of his lack of all taste for sports, children found him an enthrallingly entertaining playmate. His dramatic imagination was even enough to make him a poet—though not, by modern standards, a good one—in the bold, direct ballad style of *The Armada* and *The Lays of Ancient Rome*. It was also the Achilles heel of his moral consistency. He could not sometimes help appreciating things— people, actions, attitudes, literary works—because they were delightful and satisfying in themselves apart from their bearings on morality; nor, conversely, showing a distaste for the best intentioned efforts when their spirit or style was unpleasing or inadequate.

The dilemma came nearest to clear statement in another skirmish of the running fight with his father about literary standards. Zachary objected to his prize ode at college on *The Destruction of Pompeii*, because he had attached no moral to it.

> Is it the fact [wrote Macaulay] that no literary employment is estimable or laudable which does not lead to the spread of moral truth or the excitement of virtuous feeling? Books of amusement tend

to polish the mind, to improve the style, to give variety to conversation and to lend grace to more important accomplishments.

This is one degree in advance of the letter to the *Christian Observer*, where novels were defended only for their own (potential) moral influence. But the argument ends with a practical capitulation. 'If my life is to be a life of literature, it shall certainly be one of literature directed to moral ends.'

He could not quite keep his word. The claims of art would occasionally intrude on the majesty of moral judgment. As critic, Macaulay almost reproduces the see-saw between the wide and narrow outlook, between disinterested good taste and taste adulterated by moral prejudice, as that female intellectual, Mary Mitford, who was fourteen years his senior. The curious difference is that he never seems to have been worried by it. He could never have written, as she did, 'God forbid that I should be a canter', for such a possibility could never have occurred to him. Nor does one ever find any answer to the question he had asked his father as an undergraduate. He must, it seems, have had that faculty, more common in men of business than in artists, of keeping diverse sets of ideas in watertight compartments, and so was able to tolerate a lack of fusion that would have driven a more introspective mind to distraction. The incompatible judgments merely alternate, as if the detached intellectual and the moralist were interchanged by a switch of mental gear.

At the time of Macaulay's early manhood, the lives of many eighteenth-century personalities were being published and their letters and memoirs edited or re-edited, so that they came up for the judgment of their nineteenth-century descendants. As the most promising young contributor to the *Edinburgh Review*, Macaulay was called upon to take his share in pronouncing the verdicts of the great journal whose motto was '*Judex damnatur cum nocens absolvitur*'. Such productions were very unlike modern book reviews; they were often almost short books in themselves, and covered the life, character and works of the subject, frequently with some excursions into those of the editor as well.

At this age—about thirty—Macaulay came to the task with gusto. He was the 'most enlightened generation' pronouncing upon the less enlightened—a position emphasised by the lordly editorial 'we' of current journalism. He found much to blame in it, especially its all-too-frequent want of serious-mindedness. Boswell's lack of reticence and carelessness of his own dignity shocked him. He could only put it down to imbecility. He does not mention Boswell's reply to Hannah More when she pleaded with him to tone down some of Johnson's roughnesses, that 'he would not cut off his claws, nor make a tiger a cat to please anybody'. Perhaps she had never told him of it. Macaulay thought Boswell 'one of the smallest men that ever lived—a man of the meanest and feeblest intellect' and very naturally found it strange that such a man should have written 'one of the best books in the world'. The elder Pitt's greatness was for him marred by his theatrical mode of producing himself. While commending Warren Hastings' interest in Indian languages and customs, he said it was reserved for 'a far more virtuous ruler' to introduce to the Indians Milton and Adam Smith. He censures Horace Walpole because he cared about a pinnacle of lath and plaster more than about the Middlesex election and about a miniature of Grammont more than about the American Revolution, but adds 'no man who has written so much is so seldom tiresome', apparently unconscious that it is precisely Horace Walpole's unconventional values that make his letters so refreshing. To Macaulay, the man who wrote, 'This world is a comedy to those who think, a tragedy to those who feel', had 'an unhealthy and disorganised mind'.

His sympathy for Byron, since it could hardly be expressed directly, issued in a tirade against the society that drove him out, concluding with the famous sentence, 'We know no spectacle so ridiculous as the British public in one of its periodical fits of morality.' Less quoted is the switch-over later in the essay, 'Public opinion ought to be directed against the vices that destroy domestic happiness, but uniformly, steadily and temperately, not by fits and starts.' *

The Restoration dramatists, tactlessly re-edited by Leigh Hunt, gave Macaulay much trouble. He hated them because, unlike the coarse Elizabethan playwrights, they did not, after all, punish vice and favour virtue. Even worse, they made virtue ridiculous. The historian in him insisted that their work should be available for students; but he has little to say about their literary qualities, much more about their moral depravity. He would have no truck with Lamb's ingenious theory that these plays existed in a kind of non-moral fairyland which there was no occasion to take seriously. On the contrary, he said, they reflected, heightened and encouraged the vices of the society in which they appeared. Macaulay had retained nothing of the evangelical prejudice against the theatre and, even, in his youth, went through a phase of passionate

* Macaulay disclaims any knowledge of the nature of the quarrel between Byron and his wife. But if he had, nevertheless, picked up some rumour of it, as many people undoubtedly had, the unexpectedly lenient tone of the essay may be accounted for, since, in the repressed Victorian style, he suffered from the same misfortune—an undue attachment to his sisters.

addiction to it. If he shunned it in later life, it was merely because he was so liable to tears. But, for him, even comedies must have a moral basis.

Later in his life, when he was completely established as a writer, Macaulay refused any longer to contribute reviews on works of imagination to the *Edinburgh Review*. He owned to some incapacity in this sphere. He enjoyed reading such books, but did not want to analyse them. He would not even review Lockhart's *Life of Scott*, because this would have involved making a study of Scott's novels. In his letter of refusal, however, the moral judgment follows; he thought Scott had been 'too much a man of the world',* and therefore could not do him what the public would consider to be justice. Which of the two reasons was the deciding one remains uncertain.

At the opposite pole was his reason for refusing to write the obituary essay on Hannah More. Admitting that she had been his second mother, yet 'all the praise that I could give her writings, even after straining my conscience in her favour, would be far indeed from satisfying any of her admirers'.

A better poet than Macaulay, who was almost his contemporary, had written to Shelley about *The Cenci* —'There is only one part of it I am judge of; the Poetry and dramatic effect, which by many spirits now a days is considered the mammon. A modern work, it is said, must have a purpose, which may be the God—*an artist* must serve Mammon—he must have "self-concentration" selfishness, perhaps.' It was a sentiment Macaulay could never have subscribed to; yet he could not always refrain from burning a few grains of incense to this Mammon. The 'poetry and dramatic effect' of Plato kept him fascinated in spite of his disquietude at the Ancient Greek's acceptance

* Scott was a pronounced Tory.

of homosexual love, 'in modern times regarded as the most odious of all forms of immorality'.

Even living men, not merely works of art, could rouse this spirit in him. He loved Lord Holland, Fox's nephew, one of the most charming personalities surviving from the great days of the Whig aristocracy. 'While he lived,' he wrote in his obituary essay, 'all the great orators and statesmen of the last generation were living, too.' No one has given a more poignant description of the glory and glamour of high society in the eighteenth century than Macaulay gives in this essay and in his account of the trial of Warren Hastings. There is almost a suggestion of homesickness in them, as for some beloved country of the imagination. But there are omissions. In the essay on Lord Holland, there is barely an allusion to Lady Holland, the former divorcée, who was never received at court, but was, nevertheless, a greater personality than Lord Holland himself. Her name is not mentioned at all.

If Macaulay had lived to carry his *History of England* into the eighteenth century, he might have demonstrated an illuminating clash between the spirits of the two ages. But it seems doubtful whether, even then, his lapses from the strict moral standpoint would have become open and avowed. Most of his fellow-teachers and preachers seem never to have been troubled even by such an intermittent hankering after the old standards. The downright Harriet Martineau, indeed, saw through Macaulay. She said his History might better have been announced as an historical romance, and prophesied that new fashions would soon sweep away his fame. The prophecy would have been more aptly applied to her own work, which lacked the preservative of Macaulay's dramatic instinct.

It required in fact an earnest woman's single-mindedness to give typical expression to the spirit of the most enlightened generation. That she had, in so doing, to transgress one of its strongest taboos—against any public prominence for women—produced curious and interesting effects both in herself and in the public. It was not the only paradox in Harriet Martineau's career. Macaulay's disdain for public opinion was feeble beside hers; yet the inspiration that made her name had all the qualities of a big journalistic coup.

In 1827, when she was twenty-five years of age, someone lent her Mrs. Marcet's *Conversations on Political Economy*.

> I took up the book [she writes in her *Auto-biography*], chiefly to see what Political Economy precisely was; and great was my surprise to find that I had been teaching it unawares in my stories about Machinery and Wages. It struck me at once that the principles of the whole science might be advantageously conveyed in the same way—not by being smothered in a story, but by being exhibited in their natural workings in selected passages of social life . . . During that reading, groups of personages rose up from the pages, and a procession of action glided through its arguments, as afterwards from the pages of Adam Smith and all other Economists.

It was perhaps the only period of British history in which such an idea could have led to an immense popular success, as it was indeed probably the only period in which such a personality as Harriet Martineau's could have risen to the top. Not that it was an easy progress in its earlier stages. Harriet was a deaf, sullen, dogmatic young woman, emerged from a miserable and sickly childhood in a provincial middle-class home of 'exceedingly proper people'. There, she had been considered both stupid and bad-tempered and had been the butt of her brothers and sisters. In addition to her gradually increasing deafness, she lacked the senses of smell and taste. Her only love-affair had ended in the insanity and death of her lover. It can hardly, however, have gone very deep, since she says that her love for one of her brothers was the strongest emotion of her life. Her literary publications at the time of the great inspiration had been almost entirely confined to the press of the Unitarian sect to which her family belonged. She was delighted when they lost nearly all their money in 1829. Before that, she had been able to study and write only late at night and early in the morning, because a young lady must be seen only to sew, walk and preside at the tea-table. But, with the money, the family 'lost their gentility'. They were only too pleased, after that, to let her write as much as she wanted. None the less, in the first years after the disaster she had to rely chiefly on needlework for her keep. Convention still ruled so strongly that, even at twenty-seven, when she had a chance to work for a publisher in London, her mother ordered her home and she obeyed.

Before the idea of the economic moral tales could be realised, she had to prove herself further by winning three prizes from the Unitarians for essays designed for the conversion of Roman Catholics, Mohammedans and Jews. At last, in 1831, she was able to obtain from her family three weeks' leave to go to London, staying in a cousin's house, in order to search for a publisher for the intended series. It was not, however, a good moment to propose a new enterprise to publishers. As she trudged weary miles through London streets in December mud and fogs, having no money for bus-fares, she received always the same answer, 'The Reform Bill and the Cholera.' No one thought she could succeed. Some lectured her for rashness and presumption. Mr. James Mill disapproved of the idea. She came down to an obscure young bookseller, brother of an editor who had published some of her work without payment. He offered her the worst possible terms, with the stipulations that she must obtain 500 subscribers before publication began, and that either party could cancel the agreement at the end of any five numbers. Later, in spite of this agreement, he announced his resolve to stop the issue at two numbers unless a thousand copies were sold in the first fortnight. 'The people want this book,' said Harriet, 'and they *shall* have it.'

She describes nevertheless her own misgivings that evening.

> I began now at last to doubt whether my work would ever seen the light. I thought of the multitudes who needed it—and especially of the poor—to assist them in managing their own welfare. I thought too of my own conscious power of doing this very thing . . . As the fire crumbled, I put it together till nothing but dust and ashes remained; and, when the lamp went out, I lighted the chamber candle; but at last it was necessary to go to bed; and at four o'clock I went, after crying for two hours with my feet on the fender. I cried in bed till six, when I fell asleep; but I was at the breakfast table by half-past eight and ready for the work of the day.

In poetic justice, such heroism should have heralded a great work of science or of art. In fact, it heralded a journalistic triumph. The experts and the publishers were all wrong—as also the little whining bookseller who had driven Harriet so hard and been so unnecessarily rude about it. The public seized on the numbers as they came out with avidity, even in the middle of the Reform Bill agitation and the cholera epidemic. They were exactly what they wanted, even more so than the publications of the Diffusion of Useful Knowledge Society. Those told them about all the sciences; these concentrated on the one science they were most eager to understand, and that in a simple and easy form. Ten days after the issue of the first number, the bookseller announced that it was nearly sold out, demanded any corrections immediately and proposed to print another five thousand copies. Favourable reviews poured from the Press. Members of Parliament sent Harriet blue-books. The local Post Office demanded that she should collect her own mail. Everyone with a cause to push wrote asking her to treat it. Never, after that time, she says, had she any anxiety about employment except to choose among what was offered, nor any real care about money.

The *Illustrations of Political Economy* are plain, naïve tales of simple people in simple situations. Many of their settings are in remote places, where primitive conditions illustrate the workings of economic laws in their most elementary form. Settlers in South Africa are raided by natives, who carry off all their goods, leaving them to start again with nothing but Nature and their bare hands. Siberian tribes, living by barter, experiment with various forms of currency. A Scottish island becomes over-populated in good times and so learns, when bad times come, the value of the Malthusian doctrine. These stories, for which the author obtained local colour from books and conversation, often have a quaint Swiss-Family-Robinson charm, in spite of the interlarded chunks of economic discussion, often between the most unlikely persons. Others of the tales deal with familiar situations in English scenes, a strike in Manchester, children sent to the workhouse when their mother dies, a run on a bank in a provincial town. Harriet Martineau's imagination was prosaic, but vigorous enough within its limitations to make the stories readable. Natural catastrophes are invoked whenever necessary. The good characters are governed always and entirely by rational considerations. But, though always types, the characters are not merely good or bad; there are also the weak and ignorant, who may sometimes be reclaimed. To emphasise that the object is Instruction, that 'child of Heaven and Earth', every story ends with a summary of the economic principles illustrated.

These productions turned their author almost overnight into a power in the land. Before long, government departments (the Whigs being now in power) were begging her to write numbers in preparation for measures they meant to bring in. Lord Althorp, Chancellor of the Exchequer, consulted her about his Budget. The general public believed her to be the strongest influence on legislation and she certainly influenced some. Copies of the *Illustrations* were ordered by Louis Philippe and by the Czar, though she succeeded in offending both these potentates a little later, and the books were burnt in Russia and Austria. Meanwhile, an immense correspondence from all classes poured in. Working men of Manchester supplied her with information for her tale about the strike.

The pioneers and leaders of the most enlightened generation took Harriet Martineau to their hearts— uncouthness, irascible temper, ear-trumpet and all. Her family now made no objection to her removal to London, where she worked with grim regularity from 7.30 to 2 every day. But in the evenings she mixed with all the apostles of progress, now in their hey-day after the Reform Act—Brougham, Jeffrey, Sydney Smith, Malthus, Owen, Carlyle, besides cabinet ministers and many other politicians and writers important in their time.

Brougham took the rising of the new star well. He was furious with his Diffusion Society because they had rejected one of the stories when it was earlier offered to them and cursed them heartily that 'the whole Society, instituted for that very purpose, should be driven off the field by a deaf little woman from Norwich'. But he arranged for four supplementary tales on the Poor Laws to be issued through the Society, and used all his powerful influence to push Harriet's work. She must be almost unique in having treated Brougham worse than he treated her. She never liked or trusted him, she says, and, like many others, thought he was half insane. But then, as it appears, he either forgot or chose not to remember that he had promised to make up the Society's fee of £75 to £100, if they did not. And, so far as one can see from her *Autobiography*, Harriet Martineau never forgave anyone who had once injured or offended her.

This enthusiasm of the Radicals naturally ensured the abuse of the Tories. Croker and Lockhart planned a review in the *Quarterly* in the spring of 1833 'to destroy Miss Martineau'. They found their most promising opening in 'Weal and Woe in Garvelock', the 'Illustration' of Malthusian principles.

Harriet had been greatly influenced by Malthus' doctrine that population must be limited to match the resources available to support it; but, like her master, she had no notion of any other methods of limitation than self-restraint, late marriage, or, in extreme cases, complete renunciation of marriage, a course heroically chosen by a lover in her story. The opportunity was irresistible to the two not very scrupulous and not particularly chivalrous Quarterly Reviewers. 'A little ignorance in these ticklish topics is perhaps not unbecoming in a young unmarried lady', they wrote; but went on to suggest that perhaps Brougham had given her some information on the subject—or possibly the gentlemen 'of her sect . . . who drop gratuitous advice on these matters into areas for the benefit of London Kitchen-maids'.* The reviewers complete their attack with an unabashed *argumentum ad feminam* —'A *woman* who thinks child-bearing a *crime against Society!* an *unmarried woman* who declaims against *marriage!!* A *young woman* who deprecates charity and a provision for the *poor!!!*'

On the strength of this, the printers—for Harriet's friends were now everywhere—warned her beforehand that 'the filthiest thing that had passed through the press for quarter of a century' was coming out against her. She took the precaution of forbidding her brothers to take any action, whatever happened.

The little storm seems laughable in the modern climate of opinion, but, in those days, when delicacy in women had become a fetish, it might have meant tragedy. Many of her female acquaintances told Harriet later that, in her place, they would have gone into the mountains or to the Antipodes, and never shown their faces again. She herself ignored the whole affair outwardly and says she felt nothing but compassion for 'the low-minded and foul-mouthed creatures'. 'The testing of one's powers of endurance is pleasurable.' As for their insinuations, she did not understand them at that time, nor at any time.

The review did not confine itself to this topic. It brought out well enough the absurdities of Harriet's methods and the childish crudity of the work from an artistic point of view. But far from 'destroying Miss Martineau' it increased her sales—the inevitable result of scandal—though she regretted that, thereafter,

* Presumably some sort of advice on birth-control.

some people who had never read her books regarded her as an improper writer. However, her stoicism was justified, for all this turned out to be a side-issue. As she says herself, it was, in any case, too late to destroy her. The force that she had released—the popular thirst for economic education—was too strong to be checked even by the Pauline taboo. And yet she gave her working-class readers some bitter pills to swallow. One *Illustration* demonstrated that strikes usually left the strikers in a worse position than before. 'Cousin Marshall', on the existing Poor Laws and on charity as practised at the time, brings out the now familiar disastrous effects of doles to the able-bodied. Many philanthropists, including the famous Elizabeth Fry, sought her out after that story appeared, told her that they were now convinced that their efforts had been doing more harm than good and begged for her advice. They found that the only charities she would countenance were for education and for some slight alleviation for the old and the physically helpless. For the poor in general, her remedy remained Malthusian self-restraint, so as not to flood the labour market with more than it could support.

It seems both pathetic and admirable that the working-classes swallowed all this and asked for more. Possibly, the tone of the stories counteracted the harshness of the prescription. Without a trace of the affectation or condescension so usual in those days, this middle-class young woman from the narrowest provincial environment treats her working-class characters as fellow-creatures and gives their predicaments with an effect of participation, as if they might happen to anyone. The wretched childhood that had spoilt her temper seems to have given her a limitless sympathy for the underdog. The pale little girl dragging herself to the night-shift in the factory is no less tenderly handled because, on the author's principles, she ought not to have existed at all. Nor could Harriet Martineau, unlike the Quarterly Reviewers, ever have used 'Kitchen-maid' as a term of contempt, since all workers were worthy of respect to her. Moreover, the instruction is given as to rational beings who need only to be told the truth, and, with all its naïve optimism, this attitude frequently goes some little way to justify its own assumption.

With her politicians and her economists and her working-class following, Harriet Martineau was henceforward in the world that now counted for most. But her habits and manners remained those of a provincial prude, as she frankly confessed when a little mellowed by age and success. To anyone who met her the imputations of Lockhart and Croker must have seemed preposterous. None the less, she was inevitably courted by that fashionable world from which the glory had now departed; and accordingly we have from her an acid portrait of it in decay. The centrepiece of the fashionable *salon*, she says, was usually a gentleman on a sofa, surrounded by adorers, or a lady lecturing metaphysically and sentimentally about art, to the disgust of experts and the misleading of the ignorant. Lady Mary Shepherd was once heard to buttonhole Ricardo, the economist, with, 'Come now, let us have a little discussion about Space.' Meanwhile, matrimonial discussions proceeded in corners. Rouged and made-up old ladies paraded flirtations in the style of half a century before. Whenever Harriet found that she herself was to be 'lionised', she would leave at once, or get into a corner with a friend and defy anyone to move her—her deafness must have been an asset in such circumstances. Finally, she refused to go anywhere but 'where my acquaintance was sought, as a lady, by ladies'.

There was one exception to this ban. She would go willingly to the Miss Berrys, once the young friends of Horace Walpole, now in their eighties and still holding 'blue-stocking parties'. Apparently, they were so old, so quaint, and still so charming, that they softened even Harriet's hard realism. She forgave them the old-fashioned rouge and pearl powder, the false hair, even the 'feminine oaths' of a hundred years ago—'Oh Christ!' and 'My God!'

Harriet obviously felt an antiquarian interest in these survivors of the eighteenth century, as well as a more direct response to their charm and warm-heartedness. Rouge and powder in her contemporaries would undoubtedly have outraged her; for cosmetics had gone out, with the other graces, in the passage between the centuries, not to return to respectability for yet another century. Long before this, the one-time Mrs. Thrale had apologised for still using rouge, because it had been customary in her youth 'as a part of dress', and, as it had made her skin yellow, she could not leave it off.

Such weakenings in Harriet Martineau's rigid austerity are conspicuous by their rarity. Yet she was occasionally conscious of a lack. She lamented that she was incapable of relaxation until illness forced it upon her. In Charles Lamb, she recognised 'the spirit of geniality in which, above everything, our time is deficient'.

Ordinarily, Harriet epitomised the ungenial spirit of her time as did no one else. Though she became a complete rationalist, abandoning even the loose Unitarian doctrine of her youth—so causing a distressing family feud—a hypertrophied conscience guided every action. Truth—literal truth—was paramount for her; benevolence also obligatory, but second to it. She would not lie even for their own good to the old or sick; it seemed to her a lack of respect for them. 'A principle', she announced, 'is the most substantial and enduring of realities.' Though most of her work dealt with economic matters, she had no care to make a fortune. 'There is nothing in money that could pay me for the slightest deflection from my own convictions, or the most trifling restraint on my freedom of thought and speech.' The work itself, which brought her fame and independence, was, to her conscious self, nothing other than a pure duty.

Things were pressing to be said; and there was more or less evidence that I was the person to say them. In such a case, it was always impossible to decline the duty for such reasons as that I would like more leisure, or more amusement, or more sleep, or more anything whatever. . . . I could not have written a volume the less if I had foreknown that, at a certain day and hour, I should be struck down like Scott and Southey, and many another faithful labourer in the field of literature.

Even Harriet's friends, the Edinburgh Reviewers, considered her 'romantic' and 'high-flown' in her professional attitude. 'Romantic', as applied to Harriet Martineau, is, after all, perhaps not so unsuitable a word as it appears at first sight. Hers was a romantic story—a Cinderella story, with the public playing the part of the Prince, hailing in her the very spirit of the hard, sober, opinionated times. But such a comparison would never have won a smile from her.

Meanwhile, a fellow-worker in the field of high principle, was assailing and capturing the last stronghold of frivolity. To Thomas Arnold, Reason itself was no more than a useful tool. His table of precedence for his pupils was (1) religious and moral principle, (2) gentlemanly conduct, (3) intellectual ability. His son-in-law and biographer remarked that he was so

addicted to enunciating principles that, if he was confronted with a case that could not be immediately
classified, he would at once invent a new principle to
cover it. He could not enjoy any book or poem if he
'disapproved of the author's principles or thought (he)
was half hearted in the pursuit of righteousness'. He
lamented Shakespeare's apparent inability to create a
good man and blamed even Milton for not making
Satan wholly evil. For his boys, he wrote Greek and
Roman histories 'cleared of nonsense and unchristian
principles', a feat beside which Bowdler's achievement
pales. 'My love for any place, person, or institution,'
he announced, 'is exactly the measure of my desire to
reform them.'

Arnold was overdue when he came as headmaster
to Rugby in 1828.* The days of the first pioneers, Wilberforce and Hannah More were nearing their end.
George IV's reign was nearly over and Regency
scandals were receding into the past. Byron had died
four years before at Missolonghi. Brougham had just
founded the Society for the Diffusion of Useful Knowledge. The middle-aged Mary Mitford had published
Our Village a few years earlier; and the Princess
Victoria was nine years old. But the public schools
had lagged behind the times in spite of attacks, rising
to crescendo from 1810 on, from both Evangelicals and
Radicals. Meanwhile the public-school boys had
shown themselves worthy younger brothers of the
Regency rakes. Dr. Butler had rehabilitated Shrewsbury to some extent since 1798 and his correspondence
records some of the situations he had to deal with—
schoolboys robbing wine cellars and dead drunk on

---

* It is typical of the usual post-dating of the moral revolution
that Lytton Strachey should have included Thomas Arnold in
his 'Eminent Victorians'. Arnold lived only five years into
Victoria's reign.

the spoils, stealing ducks by means of baited hooks and lines, wild rides home for the holidays, lashing pedestrians with whips, breaking windows with volleys of stones from the top of the coaches, even shooting off a revolver at random. In 1818, a wave of lawlessness and rioting spread from one public school to another, with warnings and advice passing between the headmasters of Eton, Westminster and Shrewsbury. Not only evangelicals, but prudent people generally began to fight shy of the schools. As one critic put it, 'private schools made poor creatures, and public ones, sad dogs'. By this time, parents were beginning to prefer the former alternative; and most public schools were sinking not only in prestige, but in numbers.

Arnold altered all that. He not merely preached 'moral earnestness'—a favourite term—but exemplified it so thoroughly in his own life, that he converted his elder boys through two or three school generations before his early death in 1842. He was not so effective with the younger boys; they were frightened of him, and he was less interested in them; but his sixth form were his missionaries, allowed great authority, but weighted with equally great responsibility. He purified them drastically by sending away, without formal expulsion, any boy whom he thought to be a bad influence, even if his sins amounted to no more than carelessness or indifference. One such was despatched on the very point of honour that had made trouble between Wilberforce and his son—that of refusing to give away his schoolmates. Arnold was able to do all this, because the Rugby trustees were dismayed at the sinking of the school and had the foresight to support him through all setbacks and all unpopularity. Exclusiveness is a powerful attraction and presently the school had no room for all the boys their parents wished to send. And Arnold's methods were carried to other schools by his under-masters and pupils.

In these young proselytes, the contrast between the old and the new standards was naturally exceptionally vivid. Arthur Hugh Clough, as a poet, was exceptionally aware of it. His powerful poem, *Dipsychus*, expresses the conflicts and self-communings set up in a deep and sensitive young mind by the demands of Dr. Arnold's idealism. And, then, in the prose epilogue, an 'uncle' takes the young poet to task simply for worrying about these matters so much.

Consciences are much too tender in your generation—schoolboys' consciences, too! As my old friend the Canon says of the Westminster students, 'They're all so pious.' It's all Arnold's doing; he spoilt the public schools. . . . 'Young men must be young men,' as the worthy head of your college said to me touching a case of rustication. 'My dear sir,' said I, 'I only wish to heaven they would be; but as for my own nephews, they seem to me a sort of hobbadihoy cherub, too big to be innocent and too simple for anything else. . . . What is the true purpose of education? Simply to make plain to the young understanding the laws of the life they will have to enter. For example—that lying won't do, thieving still less, that idleness will get punished; that if they are cowards, the whole world will be against them; that if they will have their own way, they must fight for it. As for the conscience, Mamma, I take it—such as mammas are nowadays at any rate—has probably set that agoing fast enough already. What a blessing to see her good little child come back a brave young devil-may-care!'

'Exactly, my dear sir. As if at twelve or fourteen, a roundabout boy, with his three meals a day inside him, is likely to be over-troubled with scruples.'

'Put him through a strong course of confirmation

and sacrament, backed up with sermons and private admonitions, and what is much the same as auricular confession, and, really, my dear nephew, I can't answer for it but he mayn't turn out as great a goose as you—pardon me—*were* about the age of eighteen or nineteen.'

'But to have passed *through* that, my dear sir! Surely that can be no harm!'

'I don't know. Your constitutions don't seem to recover it, quite. We did without these foolish measles well enough in my time.'

But this breezy old gentleman was an uncle, and his day was over. Nor did most Rugby boys suffer as Clough did. On the contrary, it was their cocksureness that made them unpopular and their reliability that made them popular.

When they began to appear in the Universities and in the outside world, in the eighteen-thirties, the regeneration was at last complete.

LOSS AND GAIN

I am a man of peace
And the old Adam of a gentleman
Dares seldom in my bosom stir against
The mild, plebian Christian seated there.
ARTHUR HUGH CLOUGH

WHEN the old crusaders looked round on the scene of the eighteen-twenties and thirties, rejoicing at the vast improvement of society, they seem occasionally to have felt slight misgivings. Wilberforce was now over sixty, a highly honoured, almost revered figure, who, in the abolition of the Slave Trade, had achieved 'a glory purer than has ever been given to a man'.* Yet, from time to time, he lamented the decay of talent in public life, particularly in the House of Commons, 'though, on the whole, with one or two exceptions, our public men (are) better than those of the earlier part of my political existence'. There is no sign that he suspected any causal connection between the two phenomena. The ageing Hannah More, for her part, besides being appalled by the learned child, thought that the art of conversation was extinct. The classic spirit had declined with it and poetry, too, she said, except for Scott.†

But it was Mrs. Sherwood who, towards the end of a long life, described most vividly the contrasts between the scenes of her childhood and youth and those of her age.

* Mme. de Stael.
† On this last point, posterity has not agreed with her. The Romantic poets were then in full song. 'Enthusiasm' is a better stimulant to poetry than the critical spirit.

She was born in 1775 and lived until 1851, fourteen years into Victoria's reign. In her later years, she wrote her autobiography, and left also, what are sometimes more illuminating, the diaries on which the auto-biography was based.

Mary Butt's youthful semi-conversions and back-slidings have already been mentioned up to her final conversion by evangelical missionaries in India in 1807. As the daughter of a wealthy and well-born clergyman with a delightful country rectory in Worces-tershire and another good living elsewhere, she had a pleasant and care-free childhood and early youth, which her pious age looked back upon with mixed feelings. It was not, however, an undisciplined child-hood. The mature Mrs. Sherwood expresses her thank-fulness that, in her early days, her mother was a dis-ciplinarian and gave her the régime she needed. This régime even included an iron collar with backboard strapped over her shoulders nearly all day long from the age of five to twelve, and lessons recited standing in the stocks. In spite of this, she insists on the happi-ness of her childhood and, when she was free of the collar, she was a tomboy, ranging through the woods and fields around her home. She and her brother had secret haunts and private imaginative games and, when other playmates were available, used to act their favourite fairy-tales in the woods.

There were no mental stocks. She read the *Arabian Nights*, *Robinson Crusoe* and Sarah Fielding's *The Gover-ness*, from which last, in later life, she cut out the fairy-tales for a less fortunate generation of children. In curious contrast, she mentions that it never occurred to her that there could be anything wrong with the *Arabian Nights* and she allowed her own children to read it until someone kindly pointed out its 'incor-rectness' to her.

167

Later, she had the freedom of her father's extensive library and especially enjoyed reading about the Greek gods and heroes. It was a puzzle to her later how she could have ignored the 'hateful points' in the characters of these Olympians.

Mary Butt's childhood coincided with the great days of the Blue-Stockings, who had also their imitators in the Midlands, and perhaps that is why, unlike Hannah More, nearly a generation earlier, she was not merely allowed, but obliged to learn Latin. At twelve, she had to translate fifty lines of Virgil every morning, standing in the stocks, with her collar on. Her mother saw to it that she learnt her lessons thoroughly and she shot ahead of her brother, since their amiable, easy-going father was less strict with him. But her real education, as she plainly implies, was the conversation of the family and their guests. Her father, himself a lively conversationalist, had been to school at Westminster and made many friends who afterwards became distinguished in their professions, so that men of wit and intellect were constantly coming and going in their home. Many of them were naturally clergymen, and the pious old lady, writing her memoirs, feels obliged sometimes to throw in the comment that, delightful as many of them were, they did not know much more about religion than their neighbours. However, as far back as she could remember, she had assimilated naturally and spontaneously ideas of other countries, and other modes of life, such as no modern (i.e. nineteenth century) education could ever give.

Mrs. Sherwood's dislike of 'modern' education quite overrides her reluctant criticism of the unregenerate days of her childhood, and, having kept schools during most of her adult life, she had a right to an opinion. She deprecated the system of 'hurrying young minds' and lamented the precocious solemnity

of the learned child. The wisdom of her age decided
that

> Those characters who are so formed as to pass
> through scenes of temptation with the least injury
> are persons who have naturally much vivacity. . . .
> It is true that there is danger in excessive vivacity,
> but long experience has instructed me that lively
> young people in general are by no means the most
> corrupt, and that, where youth becomes corrupted,
> it scarcely ever preserves its vivacity. . . . The
> modern arrangements of society excite, without im-
> parting cheerfulness; on the contrary, they destroy
> the spring of the mind by overstraining it.

As already mentioned, in one of her moral tales, a
young girl dies of 'over-education' at fifteen.

The constant paying and receiving of visits through
pleasant country houses and vicarages over the Mid-
land countryside, the picnics and frolics and dances,
chronicled with loving minuteness in Mrs. Sherwood's
account of her childhood, encourage one to hope that
the background discipline was less continuous than her
earlier description suggests. At least, after her thir-
teenth year, discipline was relaxed owing to a change
in the disposition of her mother, who was evidently
becoming (though her dutiful daughter puts it as
delicately as possible) a nervous, self-centred valetudi-
narian. Her father, on his side, had only one point of
strictness—he insisted on courtesy to everyone, of
whatever station in life, and once sent Mary to bed
because she had shown reluctance to open a gate for
an old man with a load of wood. His Christianity was
all in the direction of benevolence and liberality.
When the dissenting chapels of Kidderminster had
collections for charity, he would attend their services
and make his young daughter hold the plate. Mary
never includes her father among the clergymen who

knew little of Christianity, as she later understood it, but one is driven to infer that in this respect he was not very different from his friends.

Mrs. Sherwood, looking back from the Victorian age, was astonished at the licence permitted to her at this time. She was even allowed to drive her mother about in a gig. Of course, there was always someone in attendance, but it was certainly 'very improper'.

In those days, Mary's family were free of the lively, cultured Lichfield circle, whose stars were the poet, Anna Seward, and the scientist, Dr. Erasmus Darwin. A frequent visitor also was Richard Edgeworth, the 'gay philosopher', who took two of his wives from the circle. But, even in her young girlhood, Mary Butt was not altogether attracted by Anna Seward, the 'Swan of Lichfield'. From a very early age she herself had had literary ambitions, encouraged by her indulgent father, and the fact that she disliked Hannah More also when she met her later, while admiring her principles, perhaps suggests a little youthful jealousy. For the diaries reveal the ferocious moralist of *The Fairchild Family* by many little touches as 'all-too-human'.

As Mrs. Sherwood in later life remembered the Seward Circle, it was not altogether what she could call correct. Anna Seward's relationship with a Mr. Saville, who was at odds with his wife, was regarded locally as equivocal. And yet—perhaps, she admits, it may only have been the glamour of youthful impressions—was there not a certain grace and charm about cultured society in those days which modern education did not foster? She cannot say whether the art of pleasing so successfully cultivated by some of the women she remembers had any solid value. As Miss Seward used it, it was of course to be condemned, and many of the Circle were no better than infidels. But even this infidelity lacked the plebian vulgarity of modern demonstrations. In this passage, Mrs. Sherwood comes dangerously near to the heresy of Burke, so execrated by the Evangelicals, when he referred to vice that 'lost half its evil by losing all its grossness'. In fact, such was the fascination of the Lichfield Circle that she could not wonder that her parents were unaware of 'the serpents that lurked under the flowers of that garden of intellectual delight'.

One small point about Anna Seward displeased Mary Butt, even at fourteen, almost as much, apparently, as the incorrectness of her ways with the other sex. This was her auburn hair, since early portraits showed that it had once been black. Even as early as 1789, it seems, opinion must have begun to turn against artificial aids to beauty. Young Mary Butt was something of a tomboy, but she would hardly have criticised in her hostess a familiar and accepted phenomenon.

There was no cramming at the school to which she was sent to finish her education, for it was the school of the French emigré, M. St. Quentin, at Reading, which Mary Mitford attended a few years later after its transfer to London, and it had no ambition whatever to turn out learned children. None the less, St. Quentin, an aristocrat of the old school, was, according to her, a first-rate teacher. But her Virgil was of little use to her here. Apart from an hour or two in the mornings, she says, the girls of the first class did as they liked. In the winter term, preparations for a dance at Christmas and the performance of French plays occupied much of the time. In the holidays, Mme. St. Quentin took Mary to London, where she saw Mrs. Siddons in *Macbeth* and they walked all day, seeing the sights, and danced most evenings. When her father came to visit her, there was more play-going and a visit to Ascot, where she saw the future Prince-Regent, 'then in the very perfection of his beauty'.

M. St. Quentin, a friendly soul, gathered round him a little colony of fellow-exiles from France and, as parlour boarder, Mary Butt had the benefit of their society and conversation. She had loved all her school-days, but her account of the last weeks becomes almost lyrical. It was 1793, and a fresh wave of refugees had followed on the execution of Louis XVI. She and the other older pupils, she says, became absorbed into their life, the ancient *vie de château*, dancing in the garden of the old abbey to harp music, receiving the gay compliments of the young French gallants with their charming manners; in all of which she never saw or heard anything amiss. For many years after, the air of a song would recall to her those 'delightfully happy days' and, when she left, she found that the girlish awkwardness that had plagued her so much had vanished and she was ready for a new social début in the country-houses of Worcestershire.

M. St. Quentin's school collapsed a year or two later, owing to his unfortunate propensity for the gaming tables, where Dr. Mitford was one of his boon companions. Then Mary Butt's father set it up again in London on the proceeds (subscribed) of her first book, in time for Mary Mitford also to finish her education there.*

The social gaieties and triumphs of Mary Butt's next few years, interspersed with what one can only call escapades, make a curious contrast with an incident of

* This was not the end of the vicissitudes of this amusing school. When Mary Butt and her eccentric godmother visited there some years later, Mary was sent to Mme. St. Quentin with a £50 note as advance payment, since her godmother intended to stay on as a paying guest. The lady promptly fainted. It was just in time to save them. The godmother then restored their finances once more.

her later life, which Mrs. Sherwood related towards the end of her autobiography. She was staying with her daughters in Nice when the officers of a Sardinian regiment, quartered in adjoining houses, pleaded in vain with her to let the girls attend a dance they were giving, for which she had given them permission to use her terrace as a passageway. None of the girls, she says, wanted her to agree, although the officers were all that was polite and deferential. It is refreshing to find that the pious family were at least able to smile when they were presented afterwards with a box of sweets having enamelled on its lid a picture of a maiden overthrowing Cupid's altar and breaking his bow across her knee.

It was these same girls who had been forbidden the *Arabian Nights* and had pleased their mother by never asking her permission to enter a ballroom. Certainly, none of them can ever have had the opportunity of causing trouble between husband and wife, as Mrs. Sherwood delicately hints that she herself once did— quite innocently—in her youth.

Any comments the autobiographer makes on this phase of her life are apt to be equivocal, if not contradictory. She does not seem to use the words 'coarseness' and 'refinement' always in the same senses. At one point she remarks that the higher ranks were very coarse and profligate in the eighteenth century; now (in the nineteenth) they are more refined. Not that profligacy is any less, but 'in a more refined and guarded manner'. In those days, there was greater ceremony, but also, on occasion, undignified romps. There was also, as she says of another visit, ease, cheerfulness and hospitality such as 'in these days we may look for and perhaps never find'. Her chief censure falls on the occasional dances and festivals at country houses, when the gentry mixed with the lower orders —traders, tenants, even servants and hop-pickers. This 'confusion of ranks' she evidently, in her Victorian incarnation, regarded as unequivocally wrong.

There is perhaps some explanation of this attitude in her account of the time when family misfortune drove her and her sister to take an interest in Sunday schools for the poor. The spirit, she claims, was very different from that of later times. There were then no plans for educating 'as it were, by mere machinery', nor was there any bar to affectionate intercourse between teachers and pupils of different ranks of society. Now, the higher ranks had been driven to withdraw by the insubordinate attitude of the lower, and control was by formality, not by friendliness. Lord Melbourne confirmed this observation when he told Queen Victoria that Lady Holland had excellent old-fashioned servants who would sometimes join in the conversation.

There was a long gap in Mary Sherwood's experience of English society when she accompanied her soldier husband to India in 1805 and stayed there with him until 1816. This must have made the changes of that period more vivid to her than to most of her contemporaries, even though evangelical influence had reached her overseas. In the meantime, she had reacted violently against native Indian life and customs; she had lost two children, since it was only beginning to be realised that European children could not stand the Indian climate, and came home mainly to save the other four; she had run schools wherever she went for children of the regiment, including even some coloured ones; and she had won fame as a writer of moral tales. Her conversion by the evangelical missionaries had been a conversion from the 'covenant of works' to 'the covenant of faith', i.e. to belief in human depravity, involving the rewriting of her *Infant's Progress* to make Original Sin the companion of the children's wanderings.

When the family came home, the mother's literary work was for a time their only prospect of support—a nervous moment, since Mrs. Sherwood says that she had never even combed her own hair for eleven years. But she need not have been afraid; by 1816, the demand for such work was immense.

Mary Sherwood's masterpiece presents the opposite problem to the writings of Hannah More. Why is it that, while a modern reader can hardly struggle through *Coelebs*, *The Fairchild Family* is still readable? It is full of sermons, scriptural texts and commentary on them; it gloats over deathbeds, triumphant and otherwise; it reiterates constantly its main thesis that 'all children are by nature evil'. The record of their punishments is enough to give a modern psychologist a heart attack—thrashing with a horse-whip (though only a 'little one'), imprisonment in dark garrets—above all, the solemn and stricken procession to see a murderer hanging in chains as a warning against anger and hate. These, of course, assist readability, but the truth is that the devil in the children is the real hero of the book, as Satan is the hero of *Paradise Lost*. Their scrapes—the natural and fatal sequence by which they are led into breaking bounds by the escaped jackdaw which keeps maddeningly just out of reach, little Harry's exploration at the new home which ends up in the pig-trough, Betsy's wild, joyous dashes through bush and briar leaving fragments of her garments behind—are told with such fine realistic gusto that the author is inevitably seen to be the unregenerate Mary Butt and not the converted Mrs. Sherwood. She did not realise that converts who have a sense of humour to keep within bounds should not risk writing even this kind of fiction.

In Mrs. Sherwood's old age, there was even an outcrop of open tolerance. She developed a doctrine of 'universal salvation', which shocked her evangelical friends. She could not believe, after all, that anyone would be damned eternally. Since she had never shown anything but horror and disgust for native India, one cannot attribute this development to any subtle after-effect of the atmosphere of Reincarnation and Karma. Rather it seems that, as second childhood approached, memories of that pleasant and easy-going, though infidel, society in which she had once mixed contrasted too painfully with the stiff and narrow limitations of the present. She even goes so far as to admit that perhaps she had been a little 'too haughty' when she used to leave the table whenever a light jest was made and that to call cards 'the devil's book' might have been excessive.

Mrs. Sherwood was an uncommonly lucky person. Unlike her children, she had the best of both worlds— the gaiety and playfulness of the eighteenth century in her youth, the work and earnestness, bringing money and prestige, of the nineteenth in her middle-age. Not that she escaped some of the intermediate travail; but the years in India, often hard and even tragic, carried her the way the world was going and ensured her future. The suppressed spirit of playfulness cropped up again only in *The Fairchild Family* and in the sparks of rebellion in the autobiography.

It was, in fact, the playful attitude to life that was lost in the transition from 1787 to 1837; and, since playfulness is said to be one of the most constant characteristics of genius, perhaps this loss has some bearing on Trevelyan's statement that the proportion of men of genius in the population of George III's England was immensely greater than in modern times.*

The individuals who remain playful in adult life,

* Obviously, such a statement cannot be based on any very exact statistics. But no one is likely to dispute it.

whether geniuses or not, are those who take delight in the arts, in fine manners and witty conversation, in intellectual speculation and achievement, who welcome new ideas, who value things and people for their own beauty and charm and not with gaze fixed on some ulterior goal. They may even value some people and things for their ugliness or grotesqueness, if it has an original flavour. Their corresponding danger is irresponsibility.

The pre-Victorians were immensely responsible people. They knew what they were after and proceeded steadily in that direction, refusing diversions. The purposes might vary somewhat, but not the grim determination. It had become the fashion to take things hard. This necessity to force themselves into a rigid mould inevitably produced psychological conflicts, often kept underground. Few were as fortunate as Dr. Arnold, whose domestic life had 'an almost awful happiness'. His pupil, Clough the poet, spoke it all out for the others in *Dipsychus*—a dialogue between the dreaming (and lazy) idealist in himself and the urge to a life of action—the equivocal, conventional life of the respectable, Church-going Victorian—which he calls 'Mephisto', but is not quite certain that it should not, after all, be recognised as the good angel. Mephisto puts the situation to him frankly—the need to adapt himself to life as he finds it, the value of 'a virtuous attachment formed judiciously' to guard one from the temptations of the streets, the necessity for polite hypocrisy, the hopelessness of keeping one's hands perfectly clean if one is to act effectively, the advantages of a professional career—with a special good word for the Church—up to the releasing lyrical outburst with its haunting refrain:

> '*How pleasant it is to have money, heigh-ho!*
> *How pleasant it is to have money.*'

Such underground conflicts in those who were profound enough to feel them make the Victorians in one sense more interesting than their predecessors. There are better stories to be told about them. Though they produced such poor drama in the theatre, they lived many dramas, not to be dismissed with a light-hearted jest, nor even to be settled in a duel or a court of law. In the eighteenth century, Mr. Barrett of Wimpole Street would hardly have expected the exclusive life-long devotion of his unlucky daughters; Ruskin could hardly have grown up without being clear about the facts of life; the ladies expert in the art of pleasing might well have seen to it that Macaulay's emotions did not remain concentrated on his sister throughout a lifetime. The Carlyles would probably have separated; the Brontes would have been impossible. All these stories would certainly have been much simpler, if they had not vanished altogether. Clough would not have puzzled whether it was cowardice or Christian meekness that made him ignore an insult. The clergymen who became afflicted with doubts would have stayed without remorse in their livings, and Darwin would have been no more execrated than his grandfather had been.

If they wrote bad plays, the Victorians wrote good novels. Fixed standards of thought and conduct gave them the solid scaffolding on which strong plots can be constructed. Thackeray grumbled sulkily that since *Tom Jones*, no English novelist had been permitted 'to depict to his utmost a man', and taunted his public that they had 'perhaps no particular objection to vice, but an implacable objection to hearing vice called by its proper name'. That it was, nevertheless, the great age of the novel suggests that the limitations were not as crippling as he supposed. Dickens, Trollope, George Eliot and the Brontes all conformed. So, in general, did Thackeray himself, both in his books and in his life. His long, weary, Platonic love-affair with Mrs. Brookfield is another story which would probably have taken a different turn, if they had lived fifty years earlier; and his novels would no doubt have lost in depth what they gained in amenity.

In other spheres, also, virtue paid dividends. Serious-mindedness and intensity of purpose bring achievement. A culture that enforces its taboos has far more drive than one that disperses its energies in universal interests, curiosity, scepticism and the critical spirit. The rising middle classes had had more of this concentration in the first place. Being endowed with set principles, they had no need to waste time in thinking about them. And there was now the new principle—a particularly useful one—the economic doctrine of Adam Smith, that for a man to push his own fortunes as actively as he could was actually the best way in which he could serve his fellow-men. If everyone did this, the law of Supply and Demand would see to it that everything worked out in the best possible manner for society in general. The men of the early nineteenth century firmly believed this doctrine. They held that there should be no social interference with economic law. The principle did not rule out Christian charity; women-folk could still distribute alms to the wreckage of economic competition. Neither did it rule out the educational campaign. The people should certainly learn, and use their education to better themselves. They should learn the economic laws, too, and then they would understand that, if they could not win the good things of life, it was inevitable and no one's fault.

The prospering classes were thus happily free from the sense of guilt which has haunted their successors in recent times. Wilberforce himself pointed out to his

children, 'How good is God to us! He gives us the
stalled ox and love too.' Even to so saintly a person,
his privileged position seemed entirely natural. He
gave away large slices of his income, but it never occurred to him to doubt his right (under God) to have
the income and the power and pleasure of distributing
it as he thought fit.

Moreover, the theory worked. In spite of the war,
and the hard times after it and the 'hungry forties', in
spite of alternate booms and slumps, the country as a
whole prospered enormously, gathering in the profits
of the Industrial Revolution with all its scientific inventions. More and more people attained a higher and
higher standard of living. The 'submerged tenth' in
the slums of the industrial towns suffered, but as this
was believed to be unavoidable, few felt remorse about
it. It was the result of the time-lag in the working of
the law of Supply and Demand—that time-lag which
the twentieth century has found intolerable.

Before scoffing at the convenience of the nineteenth-
century belief that wealth is a virtue, one must remember the other side of the *laissez-faire* doctrine—that
men should be free to pursue their own prosperity. It
led to great reforms—the freeing of the slaves, legal
and penal reform, the expansion of education, Catholic
and Jewish emancipation.* Some of these achieve-
ments would almost certainly have belonged to the
eighteenth century—they were in the young Pitt's programme of the seventeen-eighties—if it had not been
for the French Revolution and the wars. But it was the
narrowed current of nineteenth-century moral energy
that eventually carried them through. It was probably

* The Poor Law, on the other hand, though an improvement
on its predecessor, was a failure; but perhaps this is in the nature
of Poor-Laws. The success of the progressive enfranchisement of
all classes may perhaps be regarded as still in the balance.

of such matters rather than of the progress of science that Macaulay was thinking when he referred to his own as 'the most enlightened generation that ever existed'.

TWO SURVIVORS

I have described the triumph of barbarism and religion.

GIBBON

AS the nineteenth century passed on to Victoria, a gentleman of the eighteenth-century type became an oddity, but an oddity of some value and prestige. Personality of no ordinary strength was required to become neither pious, nor schoolmasterly, nor a decaying rake; or, at least, not to make some pretension to one of these rôles. But there were still a few whom rank, wealth or other happy accidents enabled to maintain the old poise. There were still survivors of the Whig aristocracy, whose suicide, in passing power to the middle classes, was a slow one; there were still well-beneficed clergymen of the jovial scholar type; even a few younger men temperamentally averse to 'enthusiasm' in all its forms and harking back to the older tradition. As they no longer predominated, and presented no danger, the old school became more tolerated and among the less rabid enthusiasts even inspired a kind of wistful liking.

Lord Melbourne, of the Lamb family that had been thought a little too rough and hearty in the seventeen-nineties, had the most interesting fate among the survivors. His political career had been retarded, partly as were all those of the Whig leaders by the long Tory ascendancy under Pitt and his successors, partly by reason of his independence and aristocratic indifference. He would not always go with his party and had no sympathy at all with its new Radical wing; he detested Brougham; he had a poor opinion of 'the people'; nor would he join the Tories, though invited, out of loyalty to his Whig connections. He once accused Wilberforce of being a very uncomfortable man to have to work with, but other people found Melbourne himself in his younger days almost equally difficult in another way. Like most political leaders of the old tradition, he was too well off and of too assured a status to pursue his political career whole-heartedly. He and his kind could afford to be fastidious. In Pitt's time, Fox and Grey had boycotted Parliament for years together, and, later, when Grey was official leader of the party, the difficulty of prising him away from his beloved home at Barnard Castle to come and take charge sometimes provoked political crises. Yet the Whigs preserved enough political strength and continuity for Grey to be the Prime Minister who finally carried through the Reform Bill of 1832. Melbourne's turn for the premiership came even later, in 1834, when he was fifty-five. So it came about that the mentor of the young Victoria when she became Queen was the man who gave vent to such un-Victorian sentiments as, 'Try to do no good and then you won't get into any scrapes', who said that a promise of support when he was in the right was no use at all—what he wanted was support when he was in the wrong, and who preferred the Church of England as being the 'least meddlesome' of the Churches.

He must have been given the measure of his task when, in one of their earliest interviews, Victoria told him, 'I have been taught to judge between what is right and what is wrong, but expediency is a word I neither wish to hear nor to understand.'

The combination of these two suggests that the Spirit of History has a sense of humour. The timing was beautiful. If William IV had lived a few years longer,

Victoria would almost certainly have found herself in the hands of Peel, the Tory leader, son of a cotton millionaire, a Utilitarian, intensely respectable and with an air of 'glacial rectitude'. If the king had died a year earlier, she—or rather, her mother, as regent—would have found Melbourne involved in the Norton scandal, a most disconcerting situation for ladies of such propriety, and it seems likely that the resignation he offered would have been accepted; whereas Victoria's elderly uncle, robustly ignoring the fact that his Prime Minister was probably quite innocent in this instance, declared that it would never do to let a political party take advantage of such 'errors of conduct', since 'we have all had our faults in this way'.

But this storm in a tea-cup was safely weathered by the time Victoria came to the throne. In the sheltered life that she had led, she may never have heard of it. For her, since she was determined to emancipate herself from her mother's dominance, Melbourne came as a natural ally as well as the pilot who could guide her through an overwhelmingly bewildering change in her manner of life.

The great difference in their ages no doubt helped also. Melbourne was not only eighteenth century, but completely mellowed eighteenth century. He was so impartially agnostic that he studied the theological works of the Ancient Fathers because the 'old fellows' were 'excellent reading and very amusing'. This was useful to him when he had to interview prospective bishops, which, however, he found so troublesome a task that he used to exclaim, 'Damn it, another bishop dead!' About one appointment, he wrote to Archbishop Whateley, 'I cannot afford to be liberal again. Would Hawkins do, and would he swallow the Shibboleth? Excuse the haste in which I write and the careless manner in which I express myself.' How little his year in Glasgow had affected him may be judged by his comment on contemporary educational enthusiasm—'If you'll only let the children alone and not always be meddling with them.'

But there was a philosophy behind his negligence and flippancy. In most instances, proposed remedies of abuses appeared to him likely to be worse than the diseases. He was much scorned by the later Victorians, when Free Trade had become established dogma, for his hesitations about the repeal of the Corn Laws. It was due to a strong misgiving about the possibility of the country's becoming dependent on foreign corn. 'Brougham says these opinions are utterly exploded', he wrote, 'but this is a way of getting rid of them equally summary, easy and satisfactory.' Most views then considered progressive impressed him similarly. The word 'enthusiasm' was by this time quite re-habilitated—both Maria Edgeworth and Mary Mitford use it in a favourable sense in their later letters, and by 1833, Dr. Arnold was reproaching a pupil for the lack of it, though he still adds 'in the good sense of the word'. But, to Melbourne, it kept its old flavour, even though the party he had to lead was seething with rival enthusiasms. He managed them like an expert horseman on a spirited horse, sometimes giving it its head, guiding it into safer courses by a touch on the rein, but quite capable of pulling on the bit, if neces-sary, as in the case of Brougham.

His answer in the House of Lords to Brougham's complaint of his exclusion from office is a typical ex-ample of his finesse. 'My Lords, your lordships have heard the powerful speech of the noble and learned lord, one of the most powerful ever delivered in this House, and I leave your lordships to judge what must be the strength and nature of the objections which prevent any Government from availing themselves of the services of such a man.'

Melbourne was the last great master of this style—the style in which Johnson signed himself to Lord Chesterfield, 'For I have been long awakened from that dream of hope in which I once boasted myself with so much exultation, My Lord, Your lordship's most humble most obedient servant, Sam. Johnson'; the style in which Pitt made his touching plea to Wilberforce from 'one who does not know how to separate your happiness from his own'. Brougham and Macaulay, however eloquent, had a very different manner of persuasion.

In the matter of style, the Victorian view that 'we needs must love the highest when we see it' is true enough; and the young Victoria was won by Melbourne's style. His was still a bluff version of eighteenth-century suavity, and this enabled him to meet the conscientious girl half-way. The adjective 'honest' recurs again and again in her diaries to describe Melbourne. At the same time, his conversation had to be a little modified. The 'damns' that occur in nearly all his sayings—so that Sydney Smith once suggested to him that they should take it for granted that everything and everyone was damned and come to the point—had to be left out when he was talking to the Queen. Only one lapse is recorded, when he was old and retired, and, on that occasion, she only laughed. With this excision, his conversation so charmed her that, after their association began, the trite little entries in her diary gradually become an almost Boswellian record of his sayings, and, though the diarist's comments are ingenuous rather than shrewd, almost as entertaining as the original Boswell.

Melbourne was soon adopted into Victoria's household at Windsor, where he spent not only much of the day, but long evenings, sitting upright, looking through albums and discussing trivialities. His old companions could not imagine how he endured it. But it is perhaps understandable that the man who had experienced the torment of marriage with Caroline Lamb should find the young Victoria refreshing. Her diary shows that she found out all that she could about Lady Caroline from other people and remarks that Melbourne had now a great horror of any woman at all eccentric or extravagant.

Their comradeship in guiding the new age lasted four years, and there was almost no jealousy or criticism over this unique situation. Occasional mistakes, of course, occurred, as when Melbourne introduced the agnostic and socialistic philanthropist, Owen, to what the *Quarterly Review* called the 'unsuspecting innocence of a Virgin Queen'. That the rigid Owen was considered likely to be offensive to virginity was due only to some theoretical views he had expressed; but the introduction was an admitted oversight on Melbourne's part. In general, responsible people were only too thankful that the Queen was under his influence. Even the Duke of Wellington, his political opponent, thought that the more Melbourne was with her the better, though he suspected that he made serious affairs a little too amusing for her. It is unthinkable that any leader of the new society could have maintained such a rôle. Such a man might well have been much nearer to Victoria in fundamental views and tastes, but his rivals would have made his position untenable. They could never have trusted his disinterestedness. As Melbourne himself said, 'The worst of the present day is that men hate each other so damnably. For my part, I love them all.'

This was the last great service that the Whig

aristocracy rendered to the nation. Whether Melbourne did anything to modify the Queen's character is problematical. According to modern psychologists, character is formed by the age of five, or at latest seven, and Victoria was eighteen when she came into his hands. At least, he found himself able to talk to her more freely as their intimacy grew. He told her that all disasters were due to awkwardness—that it was the awkward who were unlucky; that the English upper and lower classes had some good in them, but the middle classes were affected hypocrites; that one never learned anything well unless one was interested. He discussed plays and books with her. Watching a cat, he wondered what the sensation of lapping was like; he pointed out that the Maoris were cannibals because there were no other animals for them to eat. He said one should always light a fire when one was depressed, whatever the season. Discussing a reformed rake, he even told her that most people were sorry for the life that they had led, except himself. 'I was never sorry', 'which', Victoria adds, 'I told him was very wrong.' He also told her as much as was presentable about her own predecessors and rather more than Evangelicals would have approved.

Victoria usually calls Melbourne's remarks 'amusing' or 'funny', sometimes both; but it is hard to suppose that they had no liberating effect on her tight little mind. She was not in those days without the elasticity of youth. Dancing delighted her and she allowed the waltz (not yet generally accepted) though she would not take part in it herself, which abstinence Melbourne approved. She even began to read novels, though never, she says, without a sense of discomfort, and there is no mistaking her satisfaction when Melbourne told her she need not go to Church more than once on Sundays, even against the powerful influence of her Uncle Leopold. She was very much attracted by the gay gallantry of the Grand-Duke Alexander, heir to the Russian Empire, and obviously regretted that he was, for her, ineligible. So far as the situation admitted, Melbourne encouraged every expression of youthfulness. It could not go very far. The Queen had acquired a reputation for strictness almost at once; and he considered this better than that she should be thought weak. 'By God', said the gentleman he was talking to, 'they don't think that of her; you needn't be afraid of that.'

But political affairs could not wait on the idyll indefinitely and Victoria passed back to the German influences of her childhood embodied in Prince Albert the Good. Her new Prime Minister, Sir Robert Peel, after an unpropitious beginning, harmonised admirably. Melbourne surrendered his post gracefully, sending his successor some useful hints how to deal with their young mistress, who would never bear to be left out of anything, he said, but liked everything to be explained shortly and simply.

The new times had made Victoria what she was and they were with her. She suited them in her prudishness, her rigidity, her quick and confident judgment about what was right and refusal to consider any other point of view; even in the tendency to identify what she wanted with what was right. But perhaps the woman who gave her name to the age would have been even more 'Victorian', if her higher education had not been entrusted to an eighteenth-century gentleman.

Melbourne was the last great firework of the eighteenth-century display; no one except Johnson and Sydney Smith has so many sparkling *bons mots* reported of him. What he saw around him constantly provoked them. But he left no record of his own.

Except for some youthful verses, as inevitable in the society in which he grew up as was sonneteering to an Elizabethan, he was no writer; his brilliance is recorded by others. But there was also a survivor who was a writer.

Satire flourishes best perhaps in a society that is in process of lapsing from its recognised standards. There is then a vivid contrast to be pointed between what people acknowledge to be right and proper and the way they behave. When the standards are so far discarded that no educated person takes them seriously, satire becomes merely tiresome. The great satires of the eighteenth century—Pope's, Swift's, Defoe's—were written in the earlier part of it. In the later, the satirist would have been pursuing where no man fled. But there is also another period when new standards are being set up or old ones replaced which provides a fresh opportunity for the satirist. He can then contrast the new earnestness and the new taboos with the old freedom and jollity, which, of course, he will present in an idealised form.

Peacock was this latter kind of satirist. Though born in 1785, later than Brougham and Bowdler, he contrived nevertheless to have an eighteenth-century outlook. He seems to have had a native understanding of the art of living; at least, his own life presents the appearance of having been beautifully managed. Coming from a sufficiently well-off London commercial family, he had a leisured and cultured youth, in which he made himself one of the best classical scholars of the day; he undertook interesting, well-paid work in early middle-life, married at thirty-five, and retired to the country at seventy on an ample pension. He was not exempt from his share of misfortunes. His first love-affair was unlucky; his early attempts in poetry and drama were not appreciated; he lost a delightful and

much-loved little daughter and, after this, his wife became a permanent invalid. But these troubles he lived
down with rational and humane philosophy. Nature
had contributed a vigorous constitution and in youth
he was fond of walking and boating tours about the
country. Some people thought him lazy because in a
fine summer he insisted on being out all day, leaving
studies for the winter. On the top of Cader Idris in his
early twenties he 'felt how happy a man may be with
a little money and a sane intellect, and reflected with
astonishment and pity on the madness of the multi-
tude'. Evidently, this poise never left him, for, in his
old age, he was called the 'Laughing Philosopher' and
Thackeray describes him as 'a white-headed jolly old
worldling, full of information about India and everything else in the world'. His test papers for entry into
India House had been marked 'nothing superfluous
and nothing wanting'.

This spy from the Age of Reason gave his reports
in a small number of books scattered in a happy-go-
lucky manner over his long life. They fall into the comprehensive class of novels, but, apart from modern
imitations, are unlike any other novels in the language.
There are five of them in this class;—he wrote also two
historical romances not at all in the Scott tradition,
but more like the librettos of comic operas. The five
direct satires are *Headlong Hall* in 1816, *Melincourt* in
1817, *Nightmare Abbey* in 1818, *Crochet Castle* in 1831
and *Gryll Grange* in 1860. It seems characteristic that
the last, published when he was seventy-five, shows no
falling off from the wit and charm of the earlier ones.*

Peacock used the same formula for all his satirical
novels—the now familiar, but then quite new device

---

* Some critics think there was a little falling off; the present
writer can only suppose that they have been influenced by the
idea that an author over seventy must show some signs of failing.

of collecting a number of varied characters in a house-party and setting them to talk and re-act to each other. The talk predominates, but there is a light and pleasant story running through. In one or other of these books, Peacock must have given specimens of nearly every type of crank and enthusiast that existed in the age of moral earnestness. He had considerable experience of them. Though it is impossible to class him politically, he mixed with progressive circles in his youth, as was almost inevitable in a young intellectual of the time, and had certainly some radical sympathies. The poet Shelley, atheist and revolutionary, who was seven years his junior, was his intimate friend, and seems to have aroused an elder-brotherly sentiment in him—admiring, amused, humorously anxious. Peacock helped him over the disastrous imbroglio of his first marriage, receiving some abuse in return. He advised him to consider his audience in writing poetry. Later, he gently headed him off from applying for a post at India House, while adding that he would none the less be delighted to see him engaged in some practical business, 'some scheme of flesh and blood' and would do his best to find him such employment. Early death saved Shelley from this fate, if he was ever in danger; but there may still be two opinions whether Peacock was not in the right of it, especially as the first overture came from Shelley himself.

In recompense for the embarrassments in which Shelley's friends always found themselves involved, his circle provided Peacock with excellent copy. *Nightmare Abbey* in 1818 was actually written with a definite moral purpose, though not the kind of moral purpose that was usual at the time.* It was intended 'to make a stand against the encroachments of black bile'. 'The

* However, Jane Austen's *Northanger Abbey*, published the year before, was aimed at the corresponding type of prose fiction.

fourth canto of *Childe Harold* is really too bad,' Peacock explained in a letter to Shelley, who was then living near Byron in Italy. 'I cannot consent to be *auditor tantum* of this systematical poisoning of the mind of the reading public.' Byron accordingly appears in the book as the murky Mr. Cypress, and Shelley himself as the idealistic hero, Scythrop, who involves himself with two damsels, the serious and the frivolous, at the same time, and loses both. Shelley, however, countered effectually by admiring Scythrop.

Melincourt was more to Shelley's taste, since he recognised it as being 'more serious'; in other words, it satirised the people of whom he himself disapproved —politicians and economists—and glorified the natural man in Sir Oran Haut-Ton, baronet and M.P., who (being an ourang-outang) never spoke, but made most pertinent comments by his actions.

In Peacock's novels, there is always one character at least who plays the part of chorus, giving views that are obviously those of the author. Even Sir Oran has his sponsor, who makes up for the hero's silence. From serious young men in the earlier novels, like Escot the 'deteriorationist' in *Headlong Hall* who thought everything was getting worse and worse all the time until he won the heroine, these chorus characters presently become 'jolly old worldlings' like Peacock himself, the two finest and jolliest of them being the Rev. Dr. Folliott in *Crochet Castle* and the Rev. Dr. Opimian in *Gryll Grange*. These clerics were not at all of the kind that would have been approved by Wilberforce and Hannah More. Possibly they were Peacock's revenge for the charges of infidelity and abuse of the clergy made against *Headlong Hall* and *Melincourt* by the *British Critic*. Not that one can say these charges were quite without foundation, in view of passages like the following from *Headlong Hall*, where the Rev. Dr.

Gaster is upholding the doctrine that animals were created solely for the benefit of man:

'Even the tiger that devours him?' said Mr. Escot.

'Certainly,' said Dr. Gaster.

'How do you prove it?' said Mr. Escot.

'It requires no proof,' said Dr. Gaster. 'It is a point of doctrine. It is written, therefore it is so.'

'Nothing can be more logical,' said Mr. Jenkinson. 'It has been said,' continued he, 'that the ox was expressly made to be eaten by man; it may be said, by a parity of reasoning, that man was expressly made to be eaten by the tiger; but as wild oxen exist where there are no men, and men where there are no tigers, it would seem that in these instances they do not properly answer the ends of their creation.'

One can understand the irritation of the reviewer, if of evangelical leanings, at such a passage. But it seems contradictory in a long review to call the books, 'such miserable trash that no mischief could arise from them'. Nevertheless, he was right in the last clause. By this time Peacock could amuse only the few. Indeed the apotheosis of the clergy had gone so far that the publisher of his historical romance, *Maid Marion*, in 1822, thought that it had failed to sell on account of the convivial character of Friar Tuck.*

The nineteenth century was, in fact, a good time for satire, but not so good a time for the satirist. Serious-minded people do not relish witty comment. The degree of Peacock's contemporary success as a novelist measures the survival of eighteenth-century standards.

* This seems all the more curious in that the prejudice against Roman Catholicism was still very strong, having held up Catholic Emancipation over 20 years, with seven more ahead. On this point, King and people were agreed against the progressive element.

Two or three editions in his long lifetime was its limit. Compared with the works of Scott or Maria Edgeworth or Mrs. Radcliffe, his circulation was negligible. It approximated rather to that of Jane Austen, whose literary career was prematurely ending as his began. And, like Jane Austen's, Peacock's works had to wait several generations for adequate appreciation. They have only lately attained the status of classics.

In later life, Peacock recognised himself—gladly—as being behind the times. Whether or not he already recognised it when his earlier novels failed to find a considerable public, he made no attempt to alter his style or methods. His advice to Shelley shows that he did not despise popular success, but he was evidently not willing to pay the price himself. By the time of *Crochet Castle* in 1831 Brougham's campaign for popular education was in full swing, and the fun is chiefly at the expense of 'the learned friend' and 'the steam-intellect society' and 'the march of mind'.

'It has marched into my rick-yard,' says the Rev. Dr. Folliott, 'and set my stacks on fire with chemical materials most scientifically compounded. It has marched up to the door of my vicarage, a hundred and fifty strong; ordered me to surrender my tithes; consumed all the provisions. I had provided for my audit feast and drunk up my old October. It has marched in through my back parlour shutters and out again with my silver spoons in the dead of night. The policeman who has been down to examine says my house has been broken open on the most scientific principles. All this comes of education. . . . I suppose the learned friend has written a sixpenny pamphlet on mechanics.'

After *Crochet Castle* Peacock wrote no more novels until his swan-song, *Gryll Grange*, in 1860. During the intervening years he became important at India House, reporting on a projected expedition up the Euphrates, giving evidence before Commissions and organising a service of steamers round the Cape. But one lyric suggests that he did not take even these activities too seriously:

> *From ten to eleven, have breakfast for seven;*
> *From eleven to noon, think you've come too soon;*
> *From twelve to one, think what's to be done;*
> *From one to two, find nothing to do;*
> *From two to three, think it will be*
> *A very great bore to stay till four.*

This recalls the 'idleness' of Melbourne, who was always surprising people in showing as much knowledge of their subject as they had themselves.

In *Gryll Grange*, Peacock in mellow old age took a final survey of the mid-Victorian society into which he had lived, and staged a grand round-up of contemporary absurdities as he saw them. His Christmas house-party at Gryll Grange produce an Aristophanic comedy in which they use the new craze for table-turning and spirit-rapping to call up mighty spirits of the past and to show them the overwhelming glories of the present. The séance resolves itself into a contest to convert Gryllus, that follower of Ulysses who preferred to remain a swine in Circe's train, to a choice of human life again in modern times, so that

> *He may with willing mind assume his place*
> *In your steam-nurtured, steam-borne, steam-killed and gas-*
> *enlightened race.*

Hermogenes, 'the crammed fowl', who was a prodigy at seventeen, but became imbecile at twenty-five,* argues with him and is given the victory by seven com-

---

* John Stuart Mill, who began to learn Greek at three, had worked under Peacock at India House, and had a nervous breakdown during that time.

petitive examiners. Great men of the past pass before
the examiners and are all failed in their own special
subjects. But Richard Cœur de Lion loses his temper
and drives the examination board off the stage.

Reformers, scientific, moral, educational, political,
then put their cases to Gryllus in vain; the triumphs of
nineteenth-century science—ships on all the oceans,
steam trains, gas-lighted dancing-halls—pass before
him, accompanied by fires, collisions and explosions;
finally, the Popular Universal Vote, summoned by
Circe, decides that the moderns are 'wiser, happier,
better' than the men of old. But Jupiter laughs thun-
derously, chairs and tables sprout arms, rise up and
drive the spirit-rappers also off the stage.

'I almost think,' remarks Dr. Opimian elsewhere,
'that it is the ultimate destiny of science to exterminate
the human race.'

In the meantime, while the play is preparing,
idyllic love-affairs develop in the party and Lord
Curryfin, lecturer on fish for the Pantopragmatic
Society, is converted into an amiable young man in
love.

Apart from Dr. Opimian's prophecy, which has remained sufficiently pertinent, it is possible that Peacock's survey of the mid-Victorian scene was already a
little out-of-date, for, according to his granddaughter,
he rarely left home after his retirement, spending his
time with his books, his garden and the river that
flowed beside it. He could not bear anyone to be unhappy or uncomfortable in his neighbourhood; birds
were fed in the garden and guns forbidden. He detested
everything disagreeable and, in his last years, simply
avoided it. That the last survivor of the Age of Reason
should have become completely 'escapist' in the
eighteen-sixties, suggests that he had lost none of his
craft in the art of living.

Peacock was wise to retreat in his old age, but the most characteristic trait of the survivors was that they managed, after all, to enjoy the Victorian Age. In this, they differed from Victorian critics of Victorianism, of whom there were always plenty. Ruskin and Matthew Arnold assailed it with schoolmasterly scorn. Thackeray ridiculed it with a thwarted artist's bitterness. The great agnostics solemnly undermined it. The Pre-Raphaelite poets and artists assiduously poured solvent upon it. But they were, after all, Victorians themselves. They could not take it light-heartedly. The Edwardian Age, when it came, after all the efforts of the attackers, seems in retrospect a rather poor and vulgarised attempt to recover the grand civilised style; and it did not last long—was not, in fact, an 'Age' at all. Assisted by two more world wars, the tide of moral earnestness returned, though it flows now in somewhat different channels.

After all, the superiority of eighteenth-century society is acknowledged by only a few humanists. It is a question of spirit; that is, of style. Materially, that society was immensely inferior to anything more recent. The life of an aristocrat of those days would have been regarded as one of privation by a modern working-man. And even its high culture involved many casualties. If there ever comes again a time when open-mindedness, tolerance, detached intellect, a playful attitude to life, combined with artistic perception and fine manners, set the tone of society, no doubt there will again be casualties. High civilisation has to be paid for. But, as it has yet to be proved that high civilisation can exist apart from an aristocracy, it may be that we shall never again be asked for the price.

BIBLIOGRAPHY

(This list includes only books and periodicals from which specific information has been drawn. Where an authority has been used in more than one chapter, it is given under the chapter in which most extensive use has been made of it.)

CHAPTER I

Voltaire's England ed. Desmond Flower, 1950.
Annual Register (section on History of Europe), 1798.
The Life of William Wilberforce by R. I. and S. Wilberforce, 1838.
The Correspondence of William Wilberforce ed. R. I. and S. Wilberforce, 1840.
Pitt and Wilberforce ed. Earl of Rosebery, 1897.
Life of the Right Honourable William Pitt by Earl Stanhope, 1862.
Wilberforce by Sir Reginald Coupland, 1923.
Henry Dundas, Viscount Melville by J. A. L. Fraser, 1916.
Henry Dundas, Viscount Melville by Holden Furber, 1931.
Autobiography of Augustus Henry, Duke of Grafton, ed. Sir. W. R. Anson, 1898.
The Royal Fitzroys by Bernard Falk, 1950.
Memoirs of the Life and Correspondence of Mrs. Hannah More, ed. Wm. Roberts Esq. 1835.
The Letters of Hannah More by R. Brimley Johnson.
Thoughts on the importance of the Manners of the Great to General Society by Hannah More, 1809.
Coelebs in Search of a Wife by Hannah More, 1809.
Blue-Stocking Letters ed. R. Brimley Johnson, 1926.
The Life of Samuel Johnson by James Boswell, 1791.

CHAPTER II

Life and Writings of Mrs. Trimmer, 1814.
Memoir of John Charles, Viscount Althorp, 3rd Earl Spencer by Sir Denis Le Marchant, 1876.
Charles Simeon by H. C. G. Moule, 1948.
Mansfield Park by Jane Austen, 1814.
Travels in France by Arthur Young, 1792.
Life of the Rt. Hon. Spencer Percival by Spencer Walpole, 1874.
Life of the Rt. Rev. Beilby Porteus, Bishop of London by Robert Hodgson, 1811.

Practical View of the Prevailing Religious System of Professed Christians in the Higher and Middle Classes in this Country Contrasted with Real Christianity by William Wilberforce, 1797.

Scots Magazine, July 1799.

Journal of Elizabeth, Lady Holland ed. Earl of Ilchester, 1908.

The Anti-Jacobin Review, December 1805.

CHAPTER III

Letters of Lord Chesterfield to his Son (Everyman's Edition), 1929.

The Face without a Frown by Iris Leveson-Gower, 1944.

Georgiana, Extracts from the Correspondence of Georgiana, Duchess of Devonshire ed. Earl of Bessborough and A. Aspinall, 1940.

Lady Bessborough and her Family Circle ed. Earl of Bessborough, 1955.

Hary-O, Letters of Lady Harriet Cavendish ed. George Leveson-Gower and J. Palmer, 1940.

Letters of Harriet, Countess Granville ed. E. F. Leveson-Gower, 1894.

Dearest Bess, the Life and Times of Lady Elizabeth Foster, afterwards Duchess of Devonshire by Dorothy Margaret Stuart, 1955.

Diary and Letters of Madame D'Arblay ed. Austin Dobson, 1904-5.

Private Correspondence, 1781–1821, of Lord Granville Leveson-Gower, 1916.

Byron, a self-portrait (Letters and Diaries) ed. Peter Quennell, 1950.

Life of Lord Byron by Thomas Moore, 1830.

Memoirs of Richard Brinsley Sheridan by Thomas Moore, 1825.

Sheridan by W. A. Darlington, 1933.

Astarte by the Earl of Lovelace, 1921.

Life and Letters of Anne Isabella, Lady Noel Byron, by Ethel Colbourne Mayne, 1929.

The Monk by Matthew Lewis, 1795.

Glenarvon by Lady Caroline Lamb, 1816.

The Christian Observer, July 1814.

Life of George IV by Percy Fitzgerald, 1881.

Autobiography of Leigh Hunt, 1850.

Memoirs of the Literary Ladies of England by Mrs. Elwood, 1848.

The Sylph by Georgiana Cavendish, Duchess of Devonshire, 1779.

Ellen Middleton by Georgiana Fullerton, 1844.

BIBLIOGRAPHY

Hints towards Forming the Character of a Young Princess by Hannah More, 1805.

CHAPTER IV

Outlines of Moral Philosophy by Dugald Stewart, 1793
Memorials of his Time by Henry Cockburn, 1856.
Sydney Smith, Biography and Selection by Gerald Bullett, 1951.
Memoirs of the Life of Sir Walter Scott by J. G. Lockhart, 1836–8.
Edinburgh, the Golden Age by Michael Joyce, 1951.
Letters to Ivy by John William Ward, Lord Dudley, 1905.
Rhymes on Art by Sir Martin Archer-Shee, 1805.
The Creevy Papers ed. Sir Herbert Maxwell, 1904.
Lord Brougham by G. T. Garrett, 1935.
Brougham and his Early Friends ed. R. H. M. B. Atkinson and G. A. Jackson, 1908.
Lord Brougham and the Whig Party by Arthur Aspinall, 1927.
Practical Observations upon the Education of the People, addressed to the Working Class and their Employers by H. Brougham, 1825.
James Mill by Alexander Bain.
A Century of Education (Centenary History of the British and Foreign Schools Society, 1808–1908) by Henry Bunyan Binns, 1908.
Life of Francis Place by Graham Wallas, 1898.
Natural Philosophy by Henry Brougham (Society for the Diffusion of Useful Knowledge), 1829.
Political and Occasional Poems by Winthrop Mackworth Praed, ed. Sir G. Young, 1888.
Outlines of General History (Society for the Diffusion of Useful Knowledge) 1828, 1830.
Hansard, March 26th, 1923.
Life and Letters of Samuel Butler, Headmaster of Shrewsbury, by S. Butler, 1896.

CHAPTER V

Émile by Jean-Jacques Rousseau, 1762.
The Life and Letters of Maria Edgeworth ed. Augustus T. C. Hare, 1894.
Maria Edgeworth by Isabel C. Clarke, 1950.
Essays on Practical Education by Maria and R. L. Edgeworth, 1798.
Early Lessons by Maria and R. L. Edgeworth, 1801.
The Governess, or the Little Female Academy by Sarah Fielding, 1749.
The Governess by Sarah Fielding, ed. by Mrs. Sherwood, 1817.

The Guardian of Education (periodical) 1802–1806, ed. Mrs. Trimmer.
A Century of Children's Books by Florence V. Barry, 1922.
The Prelude by William Wordsworth, 1850.
A Father's Memoirs of his Child by Benjamin Heath Malkin, 1806.
John Stuart Mill by Alexander Bain, 1888.

CHAPTER VI

The Family Shakespeare ed. Thomas Bowdler, 1804.
The British Critic, October 1807.
The Edinburgh Review, October 1821.
History of the Decline and Fall of the Roman Empire by Edward Gibbon, ed. Thomas Bowdler, 1826.
Life of Nelson by Robert Southey, 1813.
Essay on the Character and Writings of Saint Paul by Hannah More, 1814.
Sense and Sensibility by Jane Austen, 1811.
Pride and Prejudice by Jane Austen, 1813.
Emma by Jane Austen, 1816.
Persuasion by Jane Austen, 1817.
Jane Austen, her Life and Letters by William and R. A. Austen Leigh, 1913.
Jane Austen, Facts and Problems by R. W. Chapman, 1948.
Life and Letters of Mary Russell Mitford by R. Brimley Johnson, 1925.
Life and Letters of Mary Russell Mitford by the Rev. A. A. L'Estrange, 1870.
Letters of Mary Russell Mitford, 2nd series ed. Henry Chorley, 1872.
Our Village by Mary Mitford, 1824.
Dramatic Works by Mary Mitford, 1854.

CHAPTER VII

Critical and Historical Essays by Lord Macaulay, 1878.
Life and Letters of Lord Macaulay by Sir G. O. Trevelyan, 1876.
The Christian Observer, 1816–17.
The Letters of John Keats ed. Maurice Buxton Forman, 1947.
Autobiography of Harriet Martineau ed. Maria Weston Chapman, 1862 and 1877.
Illustrations of Political Economy by Harriet Martineau, 1832.
The Quarterly Review, April, 1833.
History of the Thirty Years' Peace by Harriet Martineau, 1877.
The Life and Correspondence of Thomas Arnold by A. P. Stanley, 1844.

BIBLIOGRAPHY

Dr. Arnold of Rugby by Arnold Whitridge, 1928.
Poems and Prose Remains of Arthur Hugh Clough 1869.

CHAPTER VIII

The Life and Times of Mrs. Sherwood by F. J. Harvey–Darton, 1910.
Life of Mrs. Sherwood by S. Kelly, 1854.
History of the Fairchild Family, or the Child's Manual by Mrs. Sherwood, 1818.
Caroline Mordaunt by Mrs. Sherwood, 1853.
English Social History by G. M. Trevelyan, 1944.
Vanity Fair by William Makepeace Thackeray, 1848.
The History of Pendennis by William Makepeace Thackeray, 1849.

CHAPTER IX

Lord Melbourne by Henry Dunckley, 1898.
Lord Melbourne by Bertram Newman, 1930.
The Young Melbourne by Lord David Cecil.
Lord Grey of the Reform Bill by G. M. Trevelyan, 1920.
Lord Melbourne's Papers ed. Lloyd C. Sanders, 1889.
The Girlhood of Queen Victoria, a selection of Her Majesty's Diaries between the years 1832 and 1846, ed. Viscount Esher, 1912.
The Childhood of Queen Victoria by Mrs. Gerald Gurney, 1901.
Victoria by Millicent Garrett Fawcett, 1895.
Headlong Hall and Nightmare Abbey by Thomas Love Peacock, ed. (with biography) Richard Garnett, 1891.
Thomas Love Peacock by J. B. Priestley, 1925.
Melincourt by Thomas Love Peacock, 1818.
Crochet Castle by Thomas Love Peacock, 1831.
The British Critic, October 1817.
Maid Marion by Thomas Love Peacock, 1822.
Gryll Grange by Thomas Love Peacock, 1861.

INDEX

INDEX

INDEX

INDEX

INDEX

Printed in Great Britain by Butler & Tanner Ltd., Frome and London